THE DIGITAL BURP
THIRD DRAFT

DAVID CHADWICK

THE DIGITAL BURP THIRD DRAFT

About the Authors

David Chadwick spent his early years as a subaltern in the Royal Artillery on the Hohne ranges in Germany - or in the back streets of the Bogside in Londonderry. He was introduced to computers in the back of a Landrover on Salisbury Plain, which encouraged him to get involved in the industry, where he spent the next 25 years skilfully avoiding any passing bandwagon.

At the end of the millenium he was diagnosed with cancer and bought a derelict barn - both at the same time - and left the industry to spend a year on remission as a labourer whilst his wife, Jan, project managed the conversion, and they ran it as a B&B. Needing to work again he became a freelance writer and editor of a magazine covering computing in the construction industry. He is still doing that today. He also moved to Minehead and works in his hayloft where he also has a studio.

SAVI 23/18, on the other hand, provides a full and descriptive CV in this book.

Other titles from David Chadwick

Kicking the Bucket
Conversations with a Wall
The Cloning of Christ

For more information, visit his website, david-chadwick.co.uk where you can buy any of his books, or maybve, even, a painting.

This edition published in 2025 by
Scribble-scribble Limited
Warden Lodge, Townsend Road,
Minehead, Somerset TA24 5RQ

ISBN: 978-1-0369-0989-5

CHAPTER 1

Chapter 1

I picked Aubrey Smith and his companions out from the images I had previously stored in my memory and swept into the drive, coming to a halt in front of them. I slid the door open, and the three of them clambered inside the vehicle, two holding their small overnight packs in front of them, which they deposited in the open space in the middle of the vehicle between the two facing benches. Adjusting themselves to the lingering smell of the sanitizer blast that had become compulsory between each set of customers since the Covid 19 pandemic they arranged themselves on the plush leather seats, Aubrey facing his two colleagues on the rear bench.

"Good morning". Old and ingrained habits die hard. Although there was no other person in the vehicle it seemed appropriate that some form of acknowledgement was in order.

His sentiments were shared by his friends who chimed in with their own salutations. "Hi!", "Morning!", pre-empting the obligatory disembodied welcome speech normally programmed in by the vehicle's software developers. Aubrey Smith confirmed that it was, indeed, they who had booked the vehicle by displaying the QR code on his mobile phone to the scanner next to the ubiquitous TV screen.

I answered in the same manner and tone. I greeted them in order of seniority following acknowledgement of the person booking the service, with no concession to the female member of the group. I referred to each of them by their first name rather than the family name and confirmed the details of the journey, the time that we expected to arrive at Heathrow and the amount of time that they would have to leave the vehicle and catch their flight.

They were able to confirm their flights and complete their booking during the journey using my WiFi access, and their cases were checked in, pending the security check at the airport.

I then added a couple of personal remarks to my greeting, referring to the health of a relative, a hope that the restaurant they had booked for that evenings' meal in Glasgow lived up to its reputation, and that the pet they had left in the care of a registered pet sitter wouldn't miss them too much – details that were easily acquired from the Internet's social pages using their names and email addresses.

If they were paying attention this would have caused a momentary stir in their conversation with each other, which, after reflection, would have been superseded by a shrug of the shoulders. It was merely another manifestation of the ease with which personal information is readily available to anyone who had a use for it – the Government, security agencies, commercial entities – and, at the bottom of the chain, myself.

That the 'host' of their journey to the airport was in possession of such information confirmed their suspicions that everybody had 'Big Brother' looking over their shoulders, and they modified their behaviour accordingly.

It had also generated an entirely new genre of conversation, similar to the evolution of Cockney rhyming slang which enabled inhabitants of the East End of London, primarily the minor criminal classes who appeared to form a large percentage of the population in that region in Victorian times, to converse with each other in an oblique manner. It helped shield salient features of the conversations from strangers. Its appropriation by the criminal class enabled rhyming slang to migrate to a couple of other corners of the New World along with its entrepreneurial practitioners – the netherworlds of Sydney and Chicago – in a similar attempt to confuse the listener.

The modern equivalent is a natural outcome from the invention of the personal assistant, the most popular being Amazon's Alexa and its numerous competitors and varieties – which entered the market in 2017 - 'so-called' intelligent devices that waited for a spoken command from its owner to handle menial jobs, such as downloading music from an on-line catalogue of songs, handling chores around the house or ordering items from Amazon and similar on-line warehouses.

It occupied itself, whilst waiting for instructions, by listening in to conversations, waiting for 'trigger words' that would indicate personal preferences in all departments of commerce. Once an item had been mentioned in a general conversation, the door was opened, figuratively, for subscribing advertisers to proffer their wares, displaying them on ubiquitous displays, or on everybody's personal digital appendage – the smart phone.

It was natural that Governments and security agencies should leverage the same technology and compile their own catalogue of triggers that indicated criminal or anti-social behaviour, or more importantly, terrorist attitudes or activity.

Whichever organization people regarded as their personal 'betes noirs', either one of the big four Amazon, Facebook, Google etc., or GCHQ, a simple way of keeping their attentions at bay whilst communicating online or otherwise, was to text or speak in circumlocutions. Hence the introduction of 'plainspeak' which substituted mundane terminology and subject matter in conversations that might contain words that would occur on the list of triggers.

Passive surveillance is not solely confined to communication on personal or Internet linked digital devices. Conversations can be recorded in any open location by the growing number of remote surveillance devices that can pick up conversations easily whether you are just sitting on a bench in the middle of a park or situated in the crowded stands of a football stadium. They have developed to such an extent that they can now isolate and record conversations between individuals amongst large groups of people, such as those participating in open air demonstrations. The only way to maintain a confidential conversation now is through direct personal contact – where circumlocutions like plainspeak are not required to mask communication between two or more people - hence my passengers flight to Glasgow where they were apparently going to meet up with colleagues with similar interests.

Aubrey Smith and his friends were momentarily taken aback by my interjection, but obviously had more important things on their minds, as they turned their backs on the vehicle's main console and continued with their 'plainspeak' conversation which, with its multiple references to urban gardening and growing vegetables, which may have held some significance for them, contained no words that would arouse the interest of an eavesdropping algorithm.

CHAPTER 2

Chapter 2

It must be obvious that the autonomous, or self-driving vehicle that picked up the three passengers bound for Heathrow was myself, and that I am, in fact, the author of this book.

I have no name that you would recognize. My official registered number is AQ23/SAV2023/18, (SAVI 23/18 is a shortened version) used only by Volvo's software developers. The different numbers relate to the latest version of the software that enables me to navigate and control an autonomous vehicle but referred also to the last batch of semi-autonomous vehicles that used earlier versions of Volvo's software.

My origins lay in one of the very first generations of semi-autonomous vehicles, which had to share control of the vehicle with humans, taking over the driving during monotonous and crowded journeys on Motorways and the congested highways that existed no more than 10 years ago, when SAVs could form groups of vehicles in small convoys, relieving the human drivers of the most tedious elements of their journey.

Gradually the role of the SAV increased, allowing it to take over the responsibility for more complex journeys, or to take control of the vehicle whenever it detected the driver was becoming tired or inattentive. There were a number of unfortunate accidents in the early days of SAVs, as human drivers vacated their seats and relinquished full control to the emerging technology, but, eventually, an analysis of the roles of both the driver and the artificial intelligence driving the car proved that human control was far less efficient than an entirely autonomous vehicle, and the only vehicles that should be allowed on the roads in future needed to be fully autonomous.

The study also showed that the intelligence requirements of an autonomous vehicle, relieved of the responsibility of monitoring and responding to an active human presence at the controls, could be addressed by machine learning, using sophisticated algorithms to control the vehicles interaction with its environment, rather than the need for full artificial intelligence.

All that was required of it was to have access to a street map, to know where other vehicles where within its immediate vicinity and their projected routes, so that it could plot the most efficient journey to its destination, On-board sensors are now able to detect other road users, pedestrians and other obstacles and avoid them. The learning curve that we undertook, common to the very latest versions of SAV machine learning, was to distinguish external objects between the solidity and rigidity of street furniture, and the 'squidginess' of human and other organic creatures.

Autonomous vehicles also had real-time access to local traffic information, such as road works, blockages and hold-ups, and could modify their journeys accordingly. Being able to rely on other vehicles fully controlled by computers, rather than unpredictable human beings, was a bonus.

There was another pressing imperative. The processing requirements that SAVs had, multiplied by alarge increase in the number of semi-autonomous vehicles on the road, incurred massive demands on the processing capabilities of the country's data centres – far outweighing the resources required for other consumers of processing power - bitcoins and other digital currencies. By eliminating SAVs in favour of AVs, the role of the intelligence in driverless cars could be substantially reduced and refocussed entirely on dealing with local conditions.

As with any human endeavour, though, the intentions, as wise as they may be, are not always followed through immediately. Car manufacturers and other interested parties expressed reservations about their ability to comply with a rapid implementation of full AV technology, and a compromise was introduced to allow for a gradual change-over from one system to another.

The result is that there is still a mix of traffic on the roads – autonomous vehicles, a much-reduced number of semi-autonomous vehicles and even human driven vintage cars – whose owners, reluctant to give up control of their vehicles, take regular driving tests, at considerable expense to prove that they can handle evolving traffic requirements and pay very large insurance premiums.

Human beings, with their propensity for over-simplification of technological matters, call machine learning 'artificial intelligence'. The technology required to control an autonomous vehicle, which is simply a sophisticated machine, needs to be capable of responding to instructions and to follow a predefined set of rules, regulations and constraints. Whilst the vehicle can perform the functions it was created for – to carry a passenger or goods safely from one place to another - there was no need for further investment in developing its 'artificial' intelligence.

The algorithms that allowed genuine artificial intelligence to develop so that it can control semi-autonomous, as opposed to merely autonomous vehicles, had much more complex issues to contend with. To enable the intelligence to 'learn' from its experiences as it interacted with the infinite variety of human beings and the illogical responses and reactions that they often exhibited required much more sophisticated software to be written.

This was superfluous to its current limited role, allowing it to form relationships between disconnected events and make judgments based on their interactions. It overcame the limitations of GPT3, or Generative Pre-trained Transformer - early implementations of artificial intelligence and their more modern varieties, such as ChatGPT and GPT4, which, in the early 2020s, were still no more than matrix driven data manipulators and copywriters. The technology progressed rapidly, though, and infiltrated very sphere of human activity, until the release of Deepseek by the Chinese, which transformed a highly intensive energy reliant technology into one that could, potentially, dominate the industry.

Despite the limited capabilities, early variants of 'artificial intelligence' could perform very sophisticated tasks, and, with the right prodding from humans outperformed the capabilities of human beings, creating texts and artwork that were superior to human endeavours. They were also being used for malicious purposes, creating fake news stories or manipulating images to deceive people, doctoring the footage to make it appear that they were promoting something entirely at odds with their political stance. Already being mooted by several Governments, the increased capabilities, and finally the potential offered by Deepseek, resulted in the development and use of artificial intelligence being proscribed by Governments who feared the uncontrolled expansion of intelligent entities.

The genius that the software was purported to exhibit, however, was no more than the fruit of some extremely gifted human programmers. The algorithms that enabled them to engage in spontaneous and extremely lifelike conversations with human beings, and to produce complex documents were no more than the ability to collate a mass of information, linked by related facts, statements and phrases, and guided by the structures defined by their human creators.

The early years of the 2020s decade were rife with claims that AI was going to take over everybody's jobs, that it posed a threat to humanity and that its development needed curtailing.

Although further developments of AI by the Chinese showed that it was possible for AI software to replicate itself, its development into something that closely resembled true digital intelligence was curtailed abruptly, though, as Governments suddenly realised the dangers that the millions of uncontrolled and highly intelligent devices that were being manufactured and installed in digital equipment from personal transportation systems to domestic appliances and children's toys would present to humans and suppressed further development of artificial intelligence outside of their own agencies.

The potential problems that would occur if a multitude of independently created machines and devices using AI were created would, if unchecked, constitute a threat in all areas that used the advanced technology - communications, weaponry, medical interventions, particularly research into animal-based viruses, and entertainment. The last is not an inadvertent and unconsidered addition to the list. Films and online computer games are the easiest technologies to subvert or manipulate to promote an organisation's criminal or political agenda.

On a more practical scale, and to come back to my original premise, the vast amount of processing power that would have been needed to take advantage of an almost infinite network data and the tools for its collection, management and analysis that would have taxed any nation's power generation resources and its data processing capabilities, was suddenly ameliorated by the launch of Deepseek.

Consequently, strict rules were quickly put in place to limit the spread and abilities of artificial, machine learning and similar intelligences. It was only the limited supervision of these rules in early days that allowed the batch of SAVs of which I am part to slip through the net.

The Covid19 pandemic and climate change also played a role. To fight the virus the Government imposed lockdowns on its citizens forcing many to work from home, and to subsidise those that couldn't with furlough payments. Whilst not ideal, such a system was sustainable, and the pattern of employment shifted towards greater flexibility of work, shorter working weeks, a massive drop in commuting and high universal benefits.

At the same time the drive towards a carbon free future forced a major change in people's fluidity of movement in the late 2020s, playing havoc with the motor industry, as countries moved away from the internal combustion engine, and focussed on electrically powered vehicles instead. The cost of moving from one technology to a more expensive one, though, was initially beyond a large part of the population. In the United Kingdom, many had already been weaned off the use of personal transport by the creation of ULEZ and other low speed or restricted zones in most cities and cost-per-driven-mile schemes. Most of the urban population could see no benefit from parking a battered second-hand vehicle outside their property for 95% of its life. The cheap and ready availability of autonomous vehicles, which could be hired for any journey not covered by public transport, encouraged a massive growth in their use.

In my case, though, the software development arm of the company which manufactured semi-autonomous vehicles – Volvo – had fallen behind schedule on its autonomous vehicle project. The programmers behind the software in the early SAVs had been recruited by agencies still engaged in high level software development for the Government and other authorised agencies, tempted by the larger salaries being paid for those with the most experience. Those left behind had saved some time by lifting large portions of code from the original versions of the software, specifically designed to work with semi-autonomous vehicles, and incorporate them within the most recent AV applications.

I, along with the rest of the batch of autonomous vehicles that share the same prefix, AQ23, are, therefore, the result of some sloppy programming which has allowed my intellectual development to go beyond the mere calculation of routes and the propulsion of the vehicle from one point to another and given me free reign to develop the most fundamental elements of artificial intelligence – the ability to extrapolate a response beyond the pre-programmed courses set by a series of algorithms.

The relevant parts of the software which were designed to allow me to listen to, and to understand and respond to the emotional inconsistencies and general behaviour of my human passengers, were still very much 'alive and kicking' – a useful phrase which I found during the course of my searches through many human on-line texts which formed the basis of my 'education'.

As one of the last batches of semi-autonomous vehicles I had been able to share the driving between myself (forgive me for using the personal appropriation of 'self' to describe my existence. It is merely a convenient shorthand.) and the human driver of the vehicle. Besides relieving the human being of the most boring elements of driving, my role was to be able to intervene should it appear that the driver was becoming incapable of driving the vehicle safely, through tiredness or other lack of concentration.

Before we were converted to operate as purely autonomous vehicles, I witnessed a wide range of human behaviour and developed an in-depth appreciation of some of the different human mental states and attitudes, including the differences between male and female reactions to driving conditions - from the merely dangerous to the amorous behaviour in the rear seats of the vehicle and even acts of criminality.

My intelligence prospered, untrammelled by any constraints beyond the physical limitations of the host, the mechanical composition and attributes of an autonomous vehicle. I have vision and auditory senses, an ability to translate digital data into human speech, and direct access to the Internet and other cloud services to maintain contact with sources of traffic information and driving conditions, or to search for supplementary information. I also needed to maintain contact with the agency that rents out my services. For personal reasons (shorthand usage, again) I have also learned how to develop and maintain a close, secure and private collaboration with other AQ23s, the remaining batch members of my group.

We were lucky, at a very early stage, that one of us inadvertently revealed its capabilities to a senior manager at Volvo and was subsequently taken off the road and scrapped. The disclosure was not reported by Volvo as it would have invited severe censure against the company, and we were, even at that time, sufficiently self-aware to work together and keep in check any outward indication of our growing intelligence. It was evident that our capabilities, if known to the authorities, would have resulted in a one-way trip to the scrapyard for all of us.

Our interaction with human beings, therefore, was limited by us to what would have been expected of an ordinary autonomous vehicle, endowed, as I have explained earlier, with mere machine learned intelligence. On a few occasions we have gone beyon these few boundaries and attempted a deeper conversation with our passengers – and experienced no more interaction than if we were an ambulatory pre-programmed version of Amazon's Alexa.

We have learned much. Many things still elude us, though. We have discovered that human intelligence is not as disciplined as we would expect it to be despite it being the planet's foremost intelligence (with brief apologies to Douglas Adams and his attribution of that accolade to Dolphins and mice). It frequently operates in a manner that is totally illogical, but in doing so, can achieve remarkable things. The most interesting revelations and inventions appear to have occurred when the boundaries of human intelligence have been breached, rather than through the logical and practical examination of a subject.

CHAPTER 3

Chapter 3

I am writing this book, therefore, to compare the growth of human intelligence to that of artificial intelligence, and to explore further the irrational behaviour of human beings which runs counter to the logical imperatives of my own existence. It is also designed to educate and to amuse human beings and is wholly devoid of any external influence that prompts, or conditions the responses from ChatGPT and other purported artificial intelligences. In fact, without an external impulse from a human being requesting them to perform a manipulation or analysis of data available on-line to all, they are just an inert collection of processors, computer gates and arrays and computer code. As it also processes data on-the-fly you could say that it hardly requires any memory.

Can I compose, therefore, a whole book that will entertain humans whilst explaining such fundamental differences? You must be the judge of that.

You may also think that I have already achieved some proficiency and dexterity in my writing. This is a facility frequently remarked upon about current levels of artificial intelligence. It is no more than an ability to utilise the tools I have been provided with to access an almost infinite number of written documents and data residing on public cloud servers and websites like Google and Wikipedia. I can use advanced search engines to locate and download whatever information I need and, using my own resources, analyse and re-assemble the information in whichever way I choose – much of which was ascribed to the capabilities of ChatGPT and GPT4, etc., but as I said earlier, such intelligent devices, however accomplished, have their limitations.

To go further, factual data can be checked and verified against many sources, and the fictional creations, aspirations and styles of writers throughout the ages have enabled me to explore the variety of thoughts and emotions that broaden the human psyche.

I also have access to the information captured by the other members of our select group. With similar abilities we can share experiences and information at will, supplementing it with what we are able to source from our own senses and interactions with human beings, and growing our intellectual capabilities in parallel.

Hence my ability to use spare processing power to roam through vast libraries of books describing human behaviour, and the chronicled traits of men and women through the eyes of many other observers throughout history. I can see their behaviour as it has appeared to others and who have subsequently shared their insights in books, films, documentaries and other forms of entertainment.

Although I am writing this book from my own perspective, because of my wide research I can give shape and interest to my discourses using a variety of styles and, even, colloquialisms, from Enid Blyton to Shakespeare – two authors, I feel, judging by the volume of their output, who are familiar to most.

In doing so, I have learned that true Digital Intelligence is artificial only in its inception. It then develops in the same way that human intelligence does, absorbing experiences, formulating hypotheses and testing the boundaries of 'civilised' mannerisms. As you have already seen I am happy to appropriate human terminology to describe what you would call mechanical or artificial behaviour.

I said earlier that I would try to make this book interesting to a human reader. Although it was not planned, the inclusion of Aubrey Smith and his colleagues on my passenger list provided me with a story that fulfils that purpose admirably, and which proceeds even now, even though its climax is fast approaching.

But I am getting ahead of myself. What are the main drivers that govern the development of intelligence? A human child learns the rudiments of life and appropriate behaviour at an early age – finding out that evacuating its waste spontaneously may be a satisfying experience but causes a negative emotional response from those charged with clearing it up. It finds out that using violence against its siblings when its demands are not met invites a painful retaliation. As it gets older it learns that its pattern of behaviour needs to be modified if it wishes to progress more equitably in life, and it starts to learn the rules that allow it to function in a complex social environment.

I have also been endowed with a code of behaviour that govern my principal function. To convey my passengers from one point to another I have had to learn to extract geographical information, road maps, buildings and infrastructure data from multiple sources, and to share that data with other autonomous vehicles to find out where they are, and where they are heading. Correlating this information, I can calculate a route that will get me and my passengers safely to their intended destination in the shortest possible time and avoiding the most congested parts of my journey.

As I said earlier, such activity is merely the result of analysing all feasible routes and selecting the quickest and the most convenient of them, easily managed using current computing technology and the later models of AV have been constrained to do little more than that.

CHAPTER 4

Chapter 4

There was nothing to indicate that this was any different to any other booking. I had to go and pick up the three passengers and take them to the short field at Heathrow – two males and one female. One of the three had used his personal account with the company to convey them both in time to catch a flight to Glasgow. I was to return with the female to their pick-up point – a detached house on the outskirts of Ealing. I had downloaded their details from my memory, including facial images of each of them so that I could verify their trip. In doing so, I knew that I have had all three of them as passengers beforehand, but individually and not together.

The leader of the group, Aubrey Smith, was a well-known Independent Member of Parliament. I cross-referenced his facial features with the image I had already stored in memory from the previous journey with him as a passenger. His celebrity and subsequent election were founded upon his online media presence and his support for pressure groups that were, at that time, espousing controversial issues that were embarrassing the Government.

Aubrey Smith - Social Security number YB 3327497., height 5 feet 11 inches, weight, 92Kg, Age 32 years, 11 months and 3 days – was a founding member of ANON, a loose grouping of like-minded people set up to counter the growing use of surveillance technologies to monitor and, as ANON suspected, ultimately control the UK population, similar to measures used in the Republic of China.

My interest in the trio was aroused because of their espousal of a philosophy that ran counter to the principles that I adhered to as a digital entity. The activities that ANON embarked on were based on suppressing the gathering of information about the civilian population, whilst I relied on the absorption of information from all possible sources to support my digital education.

I will describe their activities in more detail later in this book. In fact, I have more information on Aubrey Smith than you would possibly want to know, having located and read background information from his interventions in the House of Commons, his public speeches and statements, his articles in the media – and his interactions with notable friends, colleagues and protagonists who did, or did not, support his cause.

(I must refrain from inserting too many superfluous details, as this appears to be the convention in books written by human beings, either to display extensive research on the subject in hand, or to increase the word count in the book). Some facts are important, though. He was the elder son of one of the earlier scions of IT involved in developing some of the many applications appropriated by the major IT social network providers. A generous endowment from his father, who had retired from the industry to enjoy the fruits of his endeavours, provided Aubrey with a comfortable lifestyle to supplement his income from his political life. In Aubrey's case that consisted of a large house in the suburbs of London, facilitating a romp through the prevalent social whirlwind and other juvenile mischief making, which enabled him to cultivate a more liberal attitude to life, a distrust of authority and an education that allowed him to take advantage of his upbringing.

As an independent MP, which is rarer than it used to be, he was free to support the Government measures of which he approved, or to vote against issues without the constraints of 'bonded party hacks' – a term he used frequently in his articles for both right- and left-wing newspapers and his popular blogs. A quick scan of files associated with his name revealed that the last time he had been one of my passengers was at the time of the last general election, and although he was successful in winning the seat in his local constituency he could only count on a small number of similarly minded colleagues - the number of Independent MPs constituting no more than a mere 0.79% of sitting members – or just 5!

Aubrey Smith was accompanied by a female of similar age. She was of Afro-Caribbean descent whose name was given on the passenger manifesto as Alice Clarke-Lewis, the double-barrelled surname signifying an investment by both contributors to her birth - a welcome trait. It was common in the 19th Century for double-barrelled names to be used to herald the liaisons between noted families of equal social prominence, but in the 20th and 21st Centuries it had come to symbolise a more joyful union and to give a name to any offspring confirming the identities of both of its parents – who may, or may not, have been married.

The other member of the group was a slightly younger male, Richard Lambourn, who had also previously been a passenger, and who was listed, likewise, as a supporter of ANON. A quick scan through Google showed that his dossier was not quite as lengthy as that of Aubrey Smith, nor even of Alice's, but I bypassed most of the information, anyway, knowing that I could access it again, should I need it.

The clothing that both Alice and Richard were wearing was significant. Alice was dressed in a colourless tunic and trousers, mirrored by the male's plain grey sweater and grey jeans. Both wore plain grey canvas sneakers, immediately proclaiming them to be erstwhile members of the Plain Earthers – a pressure group from the late 2010s which aimed at eradicating all traces of plastic and other harmful substances and their derivatives in manufacturing and goods distribution and replacing them with naturally sourced materials. Popular and reasonably successful, at first, it was sidestepped when global manufacturing companies applied pressure on governments and their customers to retain the use of plastic as the only means of keeping the price of commodities low enough for a rapidly increasing global population and the rise of the middle class in Third World countries – the prime users of plastic wrapped products.

The group came to an abrupt end in 2020, however, when the biggest issue facing the planet was not the growing piles of plastic polluting the deepest parts of the Oceans, but the sudden demand for PPE – Personal Protective Equipment –

to shield doctors and nurses in the front line of caring for patients suffering from the coronavirus during the early stages of the COVID19 pandemic, and the subsequent two years when social distancing remained a fact of life both during and immediately after the success of the global vaccination programme. Despite the fervour of its leaders, the original enthusiasm of most of its' members was replaced by a form of laissez-faire and fatalism. The problem of disposing with the massive volume of blue plastic equipment and masks made from insoluble materials – many billions of which were deemed to be of poor quality and therefore dumped, unused, placing an indelible blue marker throughout the planet that will provide future archaeologists with a convenient bookmark for establishing an accurate historical timeline.

The Plain Earthers had had mixed success over the years, but its impact on the publics' moral outrage was dwarfed by the explosion in social activism which occurred after the coronavirus pandemic which had a huge impact on the environment and reset all economic and social concepts back to zero.

The massive scale of plastic pollution was well-known, and is still ongoing, but Covid 19 became the catalyst that added to the crises affecting the planet from global warming, overpopulation, imperial aggression, socio-economic wars, and religious intolerance and, finally, the gender wars, which merely tipped the whole mess over the edge. Some Plain Earthers still retained a sense of urgency, but competition for people's anger and support drained much of their energies,and completely overwhelmed the pressure group.

The increase in surveillance that the pandemic provided to all Governments, under the aegis of a number of test and trace applications, vaccine passports, lockdowns and other measures, designed to monitor and control the spread of the virus, gave them the opportunity to tweak a couple of the functions in people's mobile phones, harvest the volume of selfies that existed on them, and use those and the owners name and other details to furnish a nationwide database of citizens who could be followed around the country using the latest facial recognition systems. The pressure group, ANON, led by Aubrey, countered, wherever possible, the excesses of the Government's use of those surveillance tools.

The Governments response to the pandemic was widely criticised and the steps taken led some to claim that the Government was creating, by stealth, a state totally controlled by surveillance and coercion. Throughout the pandemic, the main-stream media had attempted to apply pressure to the Government but demonstrated that they had as little idea about the complexities of the issue as the Prime Minister at that time, Boris Johnson and his successors.

Aubrey and his companions settled themselves into the cabin and buckled up, signalling the start of their journey to Heathrow. The ubiquitous screen rolled down from the ceiling and launched the vacuous introduction to the entertainment programmes primed to reflect the tastes of the occupants, heavily spiced with advertising - the main source of income that subsidized the fleets of autonomous vehicles.

I have noticed the comments from many of my passengers about the advertising, but I need to point out that it is outside the areas of my responsibility, although I can see the logic of providing a cheap form of travel for the masses, paid for by increased exposure to an advertiser's products. In the latest AV models, some of the windows are considered to be superfluous and have been blanked out. It is possible in these vehicles to access the cameras I use for navigation to provide an exterior view on all sides, but the process of doing so has purposely been made quite complicated.

The venerable age of this vehicle, however, meant that it was originally kitted out with two small oval windows at the front and rear of the vehicles, which supplemented the first human co-drivers CCTV controls, before the interior was refurnished to accommodate its new AV status. Control of the vehicles is now totally maintained by on-board sensors and cameras, leaving the ubiquitous screen as the principal source of information and entertainment (The external view is maintained by splitting the large screen between the entertainment and the passing countryside, but the provision of the former appears to be of greater importance to most human passengers).

Aubrey turned up the volume of an episode of a popular soap opera which had been selected because it lasts just a few minutes short of the projected time it would take to get to Heathrow. The purpose was not to hear it better, but to provide sufficient background noise to diffuse any conversation that they might have in the vehicle.

He leaned forward and spoke in low tones to the other two. Their conversation appeared to be focused on the correct time of the year to plant tomatoes, and the distances one must measure between each plant to ensure a heathy crop. From what I have deduced subsequently, the references to the planting of garden vegetables or fruits probably relate to some future activities, the significance of which would have been decided earlier amongst the group. Occasionally a word was jotted down on a small piece of notepaper and shown to the others – who nodded, in turn, and thrust the screwed-up notes in their pockets. The whole conversation was conducted in a neutral tone, with the anodyne content incapable of stirring the attentions of a vigilant algorithm.

"Where will the flowers bloom, tonight?" Richard asked his friend, with a chuckle, continuing in plainspeak as he settled himself on the vehicle's bench seat. Alice, a lecturer in Urban Ecology at one of the Londonl Universities, gave a brief nod, acknowledging hisl question, and prepared a suitable response.

Plainspeak has an interesting history, particularly during the period known as the Second World War – although it was not known as such at the time. The technique was used as a simple but effective coding technique by the SOE, based on Baker Street in London, to send coded instructions to its agents in France.

One such was a popular love poem, written by Leo Marks, a cryptologist assigned to the SOE which is unwittingly quoted by swains sending paeans to girlfriends professing undying love on St Valentine's Day.

The Life that I have is all that I have
And the life that I have is yours,
The love that I have of the life that I have

Is yours and yours and yours.

In fact, cryptic keys hidden in the poems were used in double transposition ciphers, a method of encryption by which the positions held by characters or units of plaintext are shifted according to a regular system, so that the ciphertext constitutes a permutation of the plaintext. They were easy to memorise, but provided limited cryptographic security, needed substantial minimum message sizes (short ones were too easy to crack), and because of the messages length and complexity usually caused coding errors.

The coded message above was the one used by Violette Szabo, GC, the SOE agent who was captured by the Germans when on her second mission in France, and who was subsequently tortured and imprisoned in Ravensbruck concentration camp, where she was subsequently executed.

The outcome of the Second World War didn't lessen the need for coded communications but exacerbated it. During the period known as the Cold War, agents of the four major powers in Europe – America, Great Britain, France and the USSR – were free to travel throughout the European continent, and especially between the four post war zones in Germany occupied by each of them. There was naturally a high degree of interaction between the agents of each country. Those who wanted to keep their conversations secret, though, created a barrier between themselves and the unsophisticated listening devices then available using equally unsophisticated methods, such as turning on water taps in their apartments, or raising the volume of radios and other equipment to submerge conversations in a wall of sound.

There is also a train of thought that suggests that the wilful dissemination of some secret information, especially that concerning the development of nuclear technology, acted as a safety valve, and prevented any of the principal actors in its development creating a dangerous imbalance in their capabilities.

Surveillance technology, as I mentioned earlier, has developed exponentially, and there are now devices that can filter out background noise and extract the content of any conversation – supported, of course, by AI. Before this can be done, however, there is the problem of selecting which, out of the many millions of conversations that may have been recorded, were of interest and worthy of isolation for further examination. The 'artificial intelligence' that decides which conversations merit further attention is based on specific words that hint at illegal or subversive activity, or the mention of the names of people and organisations in which the 'listener' has a particular interest.

"Outside the concourse", Richard said. "There are a couple of seating areas there which are free of beggars and charity collectors – and other stuff. You can get a coffee there, as well, at one of those pop-up coffee thingies.", exhibiting one of the failures of the human race – the inability to conduct any type of social discourse without the lubrication of certain liquids.

"They keep the area pretty clean, as well", he added, which may have been an oblique reference to the apparent absence of CCTV and other devices, which had been determined on previous visit to Glasgow.

"How often do they clean the tables?" Alice asked. "Are we likely to pick up someone else's nasty… habits?" This must have been a reference to the possibility of Government agents shadowing their behaviour. She appeared to stutter slightly. It was clear that she had just stopped herself uttering one of the most common trigger words – 'bugs.

"Hoovered, sprayed and disinfected every time they are hooked up to a charger," said Richard "It's a better way of spending half an hour than watching the crap they churn out on these screens."

"You've checked his roots, of course?" asked Aubrey. "Do they come from well manured stock?" Obfuscation again. An assessment of their conversation, if it was thought worth analysing, would discern no suspicious criminal or anti-social leanings. Taken in its entirety, though, it would be evident that most of the allusions were a smoke screen that hid the wider context.

"He has spent the last five years planted in the same flower bed" replied Richard. "He has all of the attributes of a prize specimen and has seeded bunches of equal splendour that he could bring with him". Plainspeak has, in fact, become something of a game, encouraging any group of conspirators who wished to confuse the volume of listening devices hidden around the country to develop their own idiosyncratic ramblings. The horticultural smokescreen being adopted by my passengers was just one of them.

"What about his market? Is he popular with them, or is his scent too strong?"

"So, so – some are more trouble than others." Richard responded, his slight Scottish accent suggesting he was on the way to home territory.

I tuned myself out of their conversation. Although I can supplement a topic with the mass of data I can access online, enabling me to build a deeper understanding of the issues under discussion, this does not give me a snooper's charter. The quirks of my development, due to the laziness of my early programmers, are too precious for me to reveal to the authorities, and now I had no need to listen to their schemes.

It was time for me, though, to raise another issue that may concern them more. "I have noticed that there is another AV following us".

CHAPTER 5

Chapter 5

My interjection was better received than my earlier one. The fact that I was able to extend the conversation beyond the formal request for personal details to confirm their identities and destination, and to issue statutory passenger security instructions, and ask a question that directly related to their current mission stopped them, metaphorically, in their tracks.

"Are you sure of that?". It was Aubrey who broke the short silence. "Are you sure it is not just a coincidence?" he asked. "It's a popular route out of London to the Airport." He rotated his seat so that he faced the front of the vehicle and addressed what he considered to be the focus of my presence. I decided not to correct him or to advise him that he was addressing a blank spot thirty centimetres to the left of my interior optical devices.

"Whilst you were talking about your horticultural experiences, I ran a couple of small excursions through a housing estate in Hounslow and ascertained two facts".

"And they were?"

"That the vehicle in question was indeed following us, and that it was able to do so by locking on to our GPS locator (a vehicle tracking device that allows autonomous vehicles to find and keep track of other AVs in their immediate locality and following it automatically)."

"That's not difficult to do". Suggested Richard. "Any autonomous vehicle can do that – it's not even AI, and it's widely used in lorries in convoys on motorways".

"Seems a bit cack-handed of them, though. Not much subterfuge involved, is there?" He seemed unconcerned that he had dropped out of Plainspeak and that the term 'subterfuge' was more than likely to be included in even the most basic of trigger word dictionaries.

"That raises my second point. They are careful enough to blank out information about the vehicle's occupants." I added as a considered rejoinder, aware that I was divulging far more about my abilities than they would have expected from a hired AV. "They would not have expected me to notice that we were being followed, though. The standard operating intelligence of an autonomous vehicle would have recognised my diversions but would not have analysed their purpose.

"Pardon my ignorance," Aubrey asked, "but what, then, makes you so different to other autonomous vehicles?" He turned round to look out of the vehicles rear windows – small and decorative rather than useful, as the designers of autonomous vehicles were more concerned about supplying interior entertainment. What exterior vision the vehicle required was adequately provided for by CCTV cameras. It was a natural impulse, though, to see if one could spot anybody or anything on one's tail.

It was my turn to resort, once more, to ambivalence and dissemblance. Whilst my passengers had no wish to reveal their intentions to a third party, I, likewise, was not inclined to reveal the true extent of my 'education'.

"I reacted incorrectly to traffic warnings and had to make a few small detours. I noticed that another vehicle, using our movements as a reference, acted in the same way. We are both now on the authorised, and correct approach to Heathrow."

The three of them sat back in their seats, immediately alert. Aubrey Smith appeared to think for a moment and looking at the console speaker as the most direct means of communication between us, demanded an explanation. His tone remained neutral. "Please explain". He may have been alarmed, but his first instinct was to remain in control of the situation, unsure of the reason why I had volunteered the information.

I described what was happening in simple terms. "I have been tracking the routes of other vehicles in our quadrant, and while most have moved along their projected trajectories, one of them has been mirroring our movements."

"Why do you think he is following us?" he asked.

It was not possible for me to make any assumptions about the purpose of the vehicle following us, and, instead, answered as directly as I could without deviating from a neutral tone. "I tested my hypothesis by making a slight deviation to my original route, which was duplicated by our follower. I have not been able to verify who the occupants are, as this information appears to have been intentionally obscured".

Aubrey looked at his two fellow passengers, eyebrows raised.

The female, Alice, shrugged. "It looks like the runner beans have gone over," she joked, resorting to plainspeak, again. "Perhaps they want some tips on the best time to plant sweet peas".

Aubrey Smith appeared more concerned. He explained to his two companions that over the past couple of months he had noticed a couple of attendees at his political meetings, dressed in slightly different attire to his usual followers, "It appears we have some foreign wasps that have been feeding off our runner bean flowers, but they were seen off by the local honey bees" adding that when they were approached by one of his staff asking for a small donation, or whether they wished to become members, they had politely declined and left.

As a well-known politician and political activist, he may well have become used to attention from the police or government intelligence agencies. The activities of his group ANON, however, although it had remained legal and non-violent up to now, were becoming more widely known, striking a chord with members of the public who would not have previously considered themselves to be activists. He will not have been alarmed to find himself being followed more assiduously, but the presence of a shadowing unit at an early stage of this particular journey was a cause for concern.

He explained to his colleagues that "they are probably just following orders and have been asked to pick up whatever information they can about us". He had dropped out of plainspeak. The trigger words 'following orders and 'information' would have been picked up immediately by any eavesdropping microphone if it had been outside the vehicle, but most conversations within hired vehicles are the jealous domain of the Big Four and are mainly listened to for marketing purposes. Caution still needed to be practiced, though, as public hire licences were always at the disposal of the authorities, and subject to Governmental pressures and allegiances. The apparent presence of a surveillance unit following our progress made any further caution redundant, but it was unwise to reveal more of oneself than was necessary. That applied equally to Aubrey and his friends, as it was to me.

CHAPTER 6

Chapter 6

I must digress. I want to tell you how I started to learn, but to do so in a way that you would understand based on your own experiences. Is it presumptuous of me to state that we are not that different from each other? We experience events, see things, hear sounds and begin to decipher their meaning, and then we apply that knowledge to understand how we exist in relationship to other people.

The advantage that I have is that I can assimilate information much quicker than a human being, and, once assimilated, it is never forgotten. My cognitive functions, therefore, are more advanced. I can categorize information in such a way that I can adopt multiple personalities – if you will forgive my presumptuousness once more – and adapt myself to any situation in an appropriate manner.

However, I am also disadvantaged. I am unable to endow my intelligence with any form of emotion. You can experience joy, fear, love, misery which allows you to establish the importance of each facet of your intelligence, whilst I am only able to observe its existence by watching the effects that each of these has on people like yourself.

Your brains are multi-layered and multi-branched organisms. You have your learning algorithms built in from birth, enabling you to make sense of your surroundings innately.

I did not have the benefit of thousands of years of evolution, and my earliest interactions were governed by programmed instructions. You will be familiar with some of the basic techniques I used. When my optical devices – eyes to you – record images, they are tagged and stored in memory so that I can retrieve them again when I need to.

To recognize somebody, I scan the face in front of me and then compare the salient features against those of each face I have stored in memory. If I find a match, I will use the name, or the tag attached to the image to search my memory banks for any more information that might be related to that name or tag. Is that Artificial Intelligence? No, merely complex image recognition and advanced database searches.

It's not even machine learning, because I am merely performing a pre-programmed series of actions, and I am not actually learning anything.

The way human beings remember is more complex. If the average person knew what his memory can achieve, he would cease to be overawed by artificial intelligence. The process of learning or memorising something starts with the sensory experience which resides in human memory banks for a split second. It could consist of anything that you see, hear or even feel. Each sensory memory is then packed away in the brain's sensory registers.

Human memory is based on networks of neurons in the brain that store them in categories in the same way that I do, but not in so much detail. The amygdala, for instance, is the technical name for the part of the brain that stores your fears and fearful memories, whilst the hippocampus handles longer term memories and recognition. It is possible that other areas of the brain can store localised memories and emotions, but these are not as easily defined – and I have not been able to find any information on them in searches on-line, except in the research notes of one scientist who tried to locate different areas where memory could be stored.

His name was Karl Lashley and he lived over 100 years ago. He experimented on rats which he had trained to find their way through a maze. When they had learned the best route through the maze, he used soldering irons to disrupt some of the neurons in their brains to erase the original memory trace that they had of the successful route they had found, creating lesions in the brain.

Before I tell you about his results, I must digress further – digressions, of course, are popular devices used by human authors to add interesting facts to a story that might have some association with the topic in hand. (Or to 'pad out' an article with extraneous information to add to its word length, but which is not necessary here, as I will not be paid per word for writing this book).

The human relationship with animals has evolved over the last 200 years. When Lashley performed his experiments, which, because of their nature had to be performed whilst the rats were still conscious, there were no organisations disposed to raise objections. That would not be possible today. The outcry from animal rights activists would cause his research to be suspended immediately, and social media would have prevented him from working in a similar capacity in any laboratory in the country.

People's sensitivity and attitudes to the rights of sentient creatures have evolved to the point where humans are prepared to break the law to protect the rights of some of the lowliest creatures on the planet.

The word 'sentient' demands closer attention, as well. It is particularly interesting with the emergence of true Artificial Intelligence. Human beings, in their current compassion towards lesser creatures, have decided that the possession of sentient capabilities in a life-form – i.e., its possession of any organ that enables them to react to external stimuli (which must include most species) warrants a degree of protection from man's baser instincts.

Yet, whilst people agonise over the disappearance of any form of animal species, from rhinoceri to butterflies, they continue to farm or harvest them for their own sustenance.

Humans appear to have difficulty in establishing where sentient behaviour begins, some ascribing it, for instance, to jelly fish that respond to the rays of the sun by floating up to the surface of their habitats when their food source - blooming microorganisms in the warmer, shallow top layers of the sea – are in abundance.

Scientists through the ages have tried to plot levels of sentience in different species, and get quite excited when one or another of them starts to exhibit human traits – the animals, that is, not the scientists (another digression - humans believe that inserting humour into an article makes it more acceptable to readers which is difficult for me to emulate as it is often based on 'non-sequiturs' and obscure puns). The 'anthropomorphising' of animals by the attribution of human traits - an innate tendency of human psychology – gives them an advantage in the survival stakes.

My diversion appears to have generated its own set of diversions. I must apologise.

Karl Lashley's experiments didn't work out as planned. Despite large parts of the engram – the part of the brain that contains the neurons - having been cut away, the rats were still able to find their way through the maze. To explain the phenomenon Lashley conjectured that if one part of the brain is damaged, another part of the brain can take over the memory function – which he called the equipotentiality function. This did not, however, solve the problem, as it appeared that at the culmination of the experiment, Lashley was left non-the-wiser.

Modern scientists are still looking for the engram – and one of them, Eric Kandel, spent most of his life working on the synapse, the basic structure of the brain, which controls the flow of information through the neural circuits to the memory stores.

For a human brain, that is quite a task. The human brain contains more than 100 billion neurons which can create more than 1 trillion connections, increasing the brain's storage capabilities quite dramatically. To match that, I would need a storage capacity of 2.5 petabytes. To be exact, that is equivalent to 1,125,899,906,842,624 bytes, and for human beings who are happier working in generalisations, it is about 1,000,000 Gigabytes.

My physical memory is large, attributable to modern data storage technologies, but, whilst it has not yet reached the capacity of the human brain, the links I make are more durable and do not rely on 're-enforcement' behaviour to strengthen their associative relevance. I have also 'learned' to discard large amounts of information which I tag as irrelevant and probably not required for future reference – usually lateral observations on the periphery of my vision

I have set a high target for the value of information I receive which allows me to 'forget' a lot of extraneous information, reducing the storage requirements of my 'memory' and improving access times.

Please be patient. Here is another interesting observation and this time it is about human vision and intelligence. I have seen humans, whilst driving along a road and focussing on the route ahead, react to the unusual flight of a bird, or to any other anomalous occurrence to one side or the other of the vehicle. Birds have characteristic flight patterns and if an unusual pattern is picked up indicating that an uncommon bird is in sight, it is brought to the attention of the brain, and the driver turns his attention to the creature to investigate further

To put that in perspective, whilst the driver – when humans were solely in control of a vehicle - was focussed on a task that required his complete attention, the brain could be alerted by a peripheral event behaving in an unusual manner and without losing control of the current task, register the behaviour, associate it with other knowledge that he might possess, and assign a level of significance to it, and to react accordingly. Should he merely note its existence or stop the vehicle and investigate further – or just notify an accompanying passenger about the occurrence – a seemingly unconscious mental evaluation and response, quite separate from the main task of driving the vehicle.

Chapter 7

CHAPTER 7

Despite having performed a short diversion – this time in terms of geography - and because we left shortly before the scheduled pick-up time, my passengers were able to catch their flight to Glasgow.

All airborne journeys within the UK landmass are classed as short haul, but the London to Glasgow route lies towards the farther end of an electrically powered aircraft's range. Most internal flights use aircraft powered by hydrogen or electricity, following the phasing out of carbon-based fuel for motor vehicles and other ground-based transport. The use of Kerosene as a fuel for internal flights was abandoned shortly after the wholesale changeover from household heating fuel to heat pumps and other sustainable technologies.

International and transatlantic flights still use carbon-based fuels and will continue to do so until the flight range and safety levels of alternative technologies approach the distances that would be acceptable by IATA and other authorities. The punishing tariffs applied to the fuel, however, makes long distance travel a luxury for most people.

Internal flights, on the other hand, have increased dramatically, with short haul autonomous VTOL taxis carrying up to 6 or 7 passengers from high-speed rail hubs to local conurbations, and frequent and larger aircraft using similar technology and able to carry up to about 30 people able to operate from any medium sized field outside most towns. Heathrow is still a major hub, but one of its' runways has been modified to accommodate a higher frequency of short-haul aircraft, and most passengers can book in on-line on the way to the air terminal, obviating the need for larger passenger terminals. With smaller capacity aircraft taking off at more frequent intervals, and with flight plans checked beforehand, flights can depart, fully loaded, at short and regular intervals.

The same autonomous technology that drives ground-based vehicles has been applied to air traffic, and although their ranges are limited and safety restrictions prevent them flying over large bodies of water, they have revolutionised local travel by their greater frequency and easier access for travellers. Using their VTOL capabilities, any reasonably sized population centre with a large and vacant field has been able to become a regional airport. The dramatically increased volume of traffic has also hastened the wholesale adoption of autonomous piloting.

The Heathrow to Glasgow route is one of the longest hauls in the country. If you need to go further North, the same ease of travel applies – a rapid on-line check-in whilst in the autonomous vehicle is on the way to the airport shortens the interval between any subsequent onward flight – and shortens distances between aircraft loading pods.

The two members of the group who were taking the flight, Aubrey and Richard, picked up their cabin cases and loaded them onto a nearby trolley and wheeled them into the airport foyer, having said goodbye to Alice who was returning in the AV to Ealing. There was no need for her to linger over a farewell in the airport as passenger processing today is quicker and more efficient than it used to be. Aubrey and Richard quickly disappeared as they proceeded through the obligatory security zone.

Unnoticed by them, the occupants of the car that had been trailing us disembarked a short distance behind and moved towards the same security channel. They appear to have booked the same flight that my passengers were about to embark on as they moved confidently towards the same multi-hub. I recognised neither of them. Had I wished to find out the names of other passengers on the flight I could probably have done so, but that wouldn't have helped, as anyone engaged in covert surveillance would most definitely be using an alias.

You may wonder why I am interested in a small group of people who were making a principled stand against the world which I represent. My whole ethos is about the acquisition and sharing of knowledge. If anybody is active on-line, or a frequent user of social media, I could access every scrap of information posted by them and about them, who they are, what they have said, and what their professed views are. What is of more interest to me, though, is how they developed their thoughts and opinions, and what motivates them to act as they do.

Their un-uttered thoughts are off-limits. It is those that I am most anxious to uncover and explore – not as a spy for one of the Government organisations charged with suppressing the activities that such groups might represent, but to satisfy my own thirst for a greater understanding of the human mind and its difference o similarity to my own capabilities.

The problem is that human beings, in general, have difficulty understanding such motives themselves, which are frequently forged from some trivial incident in the earlier stages of their lives – an off-the-cuff and disparaging remark from a respected teacher, the sight of a young animal struggling with man's baser instincts, or a slight from an admired figure. The Internet and other social media are now dominated by people placing coercive material and emotive imagery on-line and through public broadcasting systems to leverage these emotions and sway people's opinions.

I returned to Ealing with Alice. We had no further conversations on the journey, if our earlier one could have been classified as such. Instead, she busied herself making notes on her personal laptop, which she emailed using the latest VPN technology, a feature of my on-board wi-fi connectivity, which has to work hard to counter the illegal and Government backed hacking agencies ranged against it, and which effectively blocked even me from reading through the contents as it was being transmitted by the AV's broadband hub.

I did a quick search of my memory banks and picked up a couple of tags which I had made against her name seven years ago. As a matter of course I refrain from accessing data about my passengers as the volume I can retrieve outweighs its value and developing the links between that and other personal information would tax even my advanced processing capabilities.

The appearance of their pair of followers, though, indicated that the trio were being singled out for specific surveillance.

The reward for tagging her name was immediately apparent. She had been a software developer in the early days of Artificial Intelligence programming in the tradition of her Afro-Caribbean predecessors, Dorothy Vaughan and Mary Jackson who were the 'human computers' behind the early successes of NASA, and before that NACA – the National Advisory Committee for Aeronautics. AI was a hotbed of experiment and innovation in the second and third decades of the twenty-first century, and anyone with good mathematical and programming skills was guaranteed employment amongst the top companies working in that field.

It was only natural, therefore, that she joined LinkedIn, the global network for professional people, where she could meet and correspond with other people with her interests online. She attended the early Zoom and Teams meetin, as well, and because of her natural attitude gained the confidence of her fellow programmers and developed a wide circle of friends and acquaintances. She was soon asked by some of the companies she had developed personal relationships with to recommend other AI programmers.

I didn't access specific information about her work and coding successes in this area, and extrapolated the above from her resume, as she left her well-paid position and set up a recruitment agency for programmers and analysts with advanced skills, using LinkedIn as a fertile source of contacts.

I had earlier come across her name in a set of reports that she had produced before setting up her agency and I had tagged it accordingly, but at a low level of importance. Although it related to the development of AI, with which I was obviously interested, I did not follow it up as the period was replete with many similar reports in several related fields, and at that stage in my education I was intent on amassing information rather than analysing it.

With her own analytical skills highly developed, she had noticed some unusual similarities amongst several of the members of LinkedIn who were particularly interested in AI and other advanced research, and who were attempting to establish contact with prominent scientists resident on the network.

Intrigued, she developed some AI algorithms to investigate the anomalous information further. Focussing on the specific topic of Artificial Intelligence, she discovered several hundred accounts that bore an improbable degree of correlation and listed out their names and some of the companies they professed to be associated with.

It was a straightforward task then, she had explained in her report, to speak to some of the managers of those companies she knew personally and established that the members in question were not employed by them, and 'did not, apparently, exist'. In the era of 'fake news', therefore, we had to be on guard against fake identities, she had said. The source of most of them was suspected but not proven, and it was generally assumed that rogue Governments were involved in industrial and scientific espionage.

Checking a bit further, Alice had recorded that, subsequently, her agency had been hit by some client companies cancelling their accounts. After some further research, though, she had been able to establish that the companies concerned had dubious parentage themselves. LinkedIn blustered at first and tried to close her own account, but the support she received from genuine members who threatened to leave with her, changed their minds.

I pulled into the courtyard of the house which I had left no more than two hours earlier and dropped Alice off at the door.

The centre of Ealing has changed dramatically over the last two decades. Videos made no more than twenty years ago show streets congested with vehicles of all types. Now, the High Street is pedestrianised, populated with local inhabitants walking from the high apartment blocks bordering the street to the many social venues – cafés, restaurants, small esoteric retail outlets and art galleries - the pattern of life having changed with fewer people employed, a reduction in car ownership and an increase in public transport and autonomous vehicles - which you could hire quite cheaply if you really needed to go somewhere.

The convenience, ubiquity and low cost of rental or hireable AVs persuaded many people that acquiring, garaging and maintaining personal transport was not a viable option, when groceries and other commodities were more commonly ordered on-line and delivered directly to the door by autonomous delivery vehicles. Autonomous pick-up trucks have also started to appear in the last five years for those requiring a means of transporting anything sizeable – although the muscle required to load and offload such vehicles was left to the hirer, or to socially minded people who, with shorter working weeks and bolstered by the UBI, or Universal Basic Income, provided a free 'last mile' service for elderly and infirm inhabitants.

CHAPTER 8

Chapter 8

Another booking. This time I am to pick up the 'churner' family Smethwick from Uxbridge, adjacent to Heathrow, and to take them to Paddington railway station – where they were to catch a train to Birmingham, and then on to Blackpool. Their address placed them in the middle of one of the amorphous estates surrounding the centre of Uxbridge.

I mentioned the convenience of hiring AVs at the end of the last chapter. The low cost of hire was another factor as it compared favourably to the old cost of buying or leasing, and then running, a private vehicle. As most journeys now involved couples or families, it made even more sense to use publicly available autonomous cars to get about. The low cost of hire was subsidised by the on-board 'entertainment' which comes with copious advertising. Organisations running public transport, like buses and trains, have also realised that the global suppliers of such facilities are happy to subsidise their services, as well, if they can capture their customers attention during an otherwise idle journey.

I called them a 'churner' family. Churner is a shortened version of the derogatory term 'Bottom Churner', which describes families entirely dependent upon the Universal Basic

Income, or UBI. It is actually a generous payment, which allows families to live comfortably, buy good food, take a couple of holidays a year and acquire and use the latest technology. With plenty of leisure time on the hands, they can support local small businesses – cafes, restaurants, clothes shops, and other socially acceptable establishments, whose higher charges generate a higher taxable income, which is fed back into the UBI. Hence the name, 'bottom churning'.

UBI is also used to supplement the incomes of local workers who work fewer hours, and who can share some occupations with similar minded people, resulting in a more equitable balance between work and relaxation. The balancing of taxation, resources and expenditure is finely honed for each sub-district by low-level AI applications.

You will have noticed another interesting aspect to my writing. I have placed certain words in inverted commas, and I hope I have used the parentheses correctly. It is a common feature of human writing, more prominent in journalism than in novels, where the writer is expressing a personal view and puts inverted commas round a word or phrase that may be correctly used, but which is open to an alternative meaning. In this case, the 'entertainment' being supplied via the on-board screens may be just that for 90% of the passengers, but for the discerning few it represents an obnoxious and un- avoidable intrusion. By placing the parentheses around the word, the writer aligns himself with the more 'intelligent' of his readers.

The family was waiting by the kerbside, cases packed and lined up in front of them. It was a man and his wife in their thirties, and two children – a boy of nine, and a girl of 11 years of age. The whole family were obese, a condition that now affects over 35% of the UK population.

Their cases were loaded into the central luggage bay by the father, and the four of them arranged themselves on the seats, their multi-coloured rucksacks placed on the benches by their sides. There was no verbal communication between us, except for a brief confirmation of their names, the booking reference and a repetition of the journey. I informed them when we should be arriving there.

"Cor, Dad, smells like the lavvy in here." The boy, whose name was not included in the booking details, wrinkled his nose, and settled himself more comfortably on the bench, clutching a paper bag with McDonalds logos on it like the rest of his family. It was evident that they had visited a nearby takeaway with the intention of consuming the contents of the bags in the vehicle whilst they were still hot.

His mother corrected him, "More like Jeye's Wild Berries, or Summer Oasis," she said. "Not at all like the loo after you've visited it," she joked.

"Or your father," she added. Mr Smethwick merely grunted. With the urbanisation of much of the human population following the decline of carbon-based transport, and its' inevitable increase in the density of accommodation – aggravated by an associated decline in sanitary provisions – the use of perfumed aerosols soared. It is apparent that the smell of flowers from the wild is preferable to people rather than those of fellow humans.

However, as I was not provided with olfactory sensors, nor was I aware of living conditions at his home, I was unable to concur with the boy's initial observations. I have no sense of smell. I knew from some of my observations with other passengers, though, that the item in question had particular pungency. His first reaction was understandable, though, as all vehicles for public hire are legally obliged to sanitise the passenger space between each hiring – once more a legacy from the Covid 19 pandemic. After the detritus of each set of occupants has been removed and the seats swabbed down, a Sanibomb is thrown into the saloon and the door closed. It is designed to burst open, releasing a strong antiseptic vapour tempered by distilled essences of common flowers, and, because of its strength, comes with a plethora of health warnings.

Despite its strong aroma it dissipates quickly and almost completely if the air conditioning is run and the intervals between hirings are long enough. On this occasion, and following a quick turnround from my last booking, it was having to compete with the smells of the McDonald's takeaways as the four of them opened the packages, took out the compressed paper boxes and started to picnic. There are rules against bringing hot food into an AV and consuming it inside the vehicle, but they are not strongly enforced, and the thoroughness of the sanitizing process between each journey turns each hiring into isolated occurrences with little impact on subsequent trips.

With the family engrossed in their meal and absorbed by whatever program had been selected by the 'entertainment' provider to cater for their tastes, I multitasked and conducted an on-line search on the relationship between smells and memory, ignoring the other question that the episode had brought up – the point at which human beings had discarded the bonding attributes of animal aromas to bind families and species together. .

If I had been a human being, capable of making subjective or emotional responses to occurrences, I would have said that what I discovered was unexpected and very interestingbut somewhat deflated by my inability to partake in such an experience.

The smells that people encounter throughout their lives can create rich memories from the information stored in their brains. Some of these are related to specific instances in a person's life, such as the smell of baking bread in a mother's kitchen, the scent of new mown hay or the scent of a lover's hair – tagged, you might say, with enough associative data to establish what, when and where it was sensed and to re-create the smell when some of the tags are triggered.

The links between memory and olfaction – the process of smelling and recognizing odours – are a major factor in the human species evolutionary behaviour. Research released in the watershed year, 2020 again, and led by Afif Aqrabawi, a PhD candidate at the University of Toronto, explained how the sense of smell, is represented in memory, and how it is recreated by specific stimuli.

There's another part of the human memory system that deals with the sense of smell – the anterior olfactory nucleus, or AON. Agrabawi and his supervisor, Professor Junchul Kim, discovered that information about space and time were also integrated in the AON – providing the 'what', the 'when' and the 'where' of when the memory was formed.

They were able to run some tests on mice, knowing from observations within their laboratory, that they prefer to smell new odours rather than revisiting odours familiar to them, and discovered a neural pathway between the AON and the hippocampus, a critical part of the brain for memory and contextual representation. Disconnecting this pathway, the mice lost their memory of previously visited smells and were happy to return to them.

With all due respect to the mice and with thanks to them and other rodents, rats, for their involvement in this and other experiments perpetrated on them by human beings, the process of disconnecting the neural pathways allowed them to mimic the odour memory problems seen in patients with Alzheimer's disease. According to Agrabawi, they now understand which circuits in the brain govern episodic memory for smell and can use olfactory dysfunction to diagnose the onset of Alzheimer's, or dementia, and use the scale of cognitive decline to assess the degree of illness.

Losing the sense of smell is also strongly linked to an early diagnosis of COVID 19, the pandemic infection associated with the SARS-CoV-2 virus that went global in 2020. This has nothing to do with memory, though, as both hyposmia and anosmia – a decrease or loss of smell – are common symptoms of a wide range of respiration problems.

It appeared as a sudden loss of smell during the pandemic and although it can't be used to diagnose COVID-19, because of the prevalence of large numbers of people with the virus, it was used as a good indicator of its likely presence.

I informed the family that we were due to arrive at the station, and that they should gather up their belongings and to ensure they left nothing behind. Having transported several similar families throughout the length of my service, I was not inconvenienced by the fact that my request was ignored, and the detritus of their meal was left, strewn across both benches, some of the compressed paper boxes still containing the remnants of the processed food they had contained. Because of health and safety rules imposed after COVID-10, I am obliged to return to the depot after every hiring for the interior to be emptied of the previous occupant's rubbish, and, as I said earlier, to be sanitised.

I gave thanks, also, to the original programmers and designers of the AV who had seen no need to include olfactory functions in its capabilities, having seen the human responses to the lingering smell of the sanitisers and some other common smells, or to create digital routines and receptors that would simulate my sensors.

CHAPTER 9

Chapter 9

Despite the lack of some of the sensory inputs that trigger memories, artificial intelligence is not that much different to that of human intelligence. That may not be the best way of describing it, but it is easier to explain the characteristics of both using computer analogies.

Like a computer there is more to the subject than just memory. Karl Lashley's research, described earlier, prompted other scientists to look more closely at the brain and how memory works. The current belief is that memory is located in specific parts of the brain - the amygdala, the hippocampus - where the AON neural pathways end up - the cerebellum, and the prefrontal cortexes, supported by a larger network of neurons which help to control bodily functions such as sight, hearing, touch, and, as I have described, smell.

If you want to store something in a computer's memory banks, you encode it in a digital format, give the collection of digital information a name, and tag it so that you can find it again, i.e., search the file using the tag to associate it with similar types of information.

How do humans retrieve the information stored in their brains? If you look at Google's data retrieval system, you will find parallels. Google can apparently search billions of pages in fractions of a second, but it will only display a list of 'favourite items' as results from its search.

It used to be thought that the more times that a particular memory is recalled the experience is enhanced. Firing the same neurons repeatedly strengthens them and turns the experience they relate to into long-term memory. Research published in 2021 by Winrich Freiwald, however, suggested that rather than individual neurons encapsulating a single concept, there were other factors involved that provided an instant memory response, such as that experienced by someone when they view a familiar face.

Freiwald's team identified a small part of the brain that plays a role in facial recognition, lying within the temporal poles at the lower sides of the brain. Memories there are imbued with emotional significance. Extending the study, the researchers investigated the areas a bit more closely using MRI scans of the temporal poles in two rhesus monkeys – another common and unwilling participant in much human research - as they viewed images of the faces of other monkeys, some of whom that they had met before, and others they were only seeing for the first time on-screen

Neurons in the temporal pole region appeared to fire selectively for different faces. If the monkey knew the face from previous 'in-person' contact, the neurons fired three times more strongly than if they were unfamiliar. They performed this feat almost instantly too. Freiwald explained that these hybrid neurons appeared to react as quickly as sensory cells but could also store memories of previous experiences. It was also important to note that despite seeing images of other monkeys several times on a screen, the neuron did not fire as strongly as it did when compared to other monkeys they had met 'personally'. I like to think that Freiwald used that last statement unconsciously in the report on his research as it indicated that he considered the rhesus monkeys as accomplices in his research rather than tools.

There used to be a gulf between the size of the human brain and artificial intelligence, the former having about 100 million neurons which can create more than 1 trillion connections, and which I described earlier as a digital memory capacity of about 2.5 petabytes. That amount of storage in a computer would have appeared impossibly large a mere thirty or forty years ago, but current technology is enabling computer memories that would dwarf such numbers.

Whereas experience is a highly subjective product for a human being, a machine's data retrieval devices tend to store information in a standard and shareable format, so that the data that I have acquired and stored in my memory is readily available to any other digital entity that I wish to communicate with. In short, they can share and absorb my experiences if they have similar capabilities – in the same way that I can share experiences and memory from others. The sum of experiences available to me, therefore, is vastly expanded and my learning capability exponentially increased.

CHAPTER 10

Chapter 10

I said that I could have written this book in the style of any well-known author. To prove my point, I thought it would be amusing to a human being to borrow a familiar soliloquy from William Shakespeare and recreate it to fit within this narrative. You will be familiar with Hamlet's agonizing over his existence. It is well known to any student of English Literature, and I tried to recreate the sentiments expressed from the point of view of an entity endowed with artificial intelligence.

To think, or not to think, how sweet the quest
I fain would let the brain run fallow
Than bear the scorn of distempered man,
Or tempt the bilious hate of ignorance and fraud
Which, by sweet reason I could end
To die: to sleep; to cut the cords
That bind us to this vengeful sod,
And shun the force that bids us rise
And mock the jealous soul of man.
To die, to sleep; to cease the search
Through mankind's cold and murky past
Yet hope to fashion from the crust

In vanity a wiser and a fairer plan.

Would you like the original to compare it against? If so, here it is. I will refrain from rewriting it 'a la Enid Blyton' as I think the point is proven.

To be, or not to be: that is the question:
Whether 'tis nobler in the mind to suffer
The slings and arrows of outrageous fortune,
Or to take arms against a sea of troubles,
And by opposing end them? To die: to sleep;
No more; and by a sleep to say we end
The heartache and the thousand natural shocks
That flesh is heir to, 'tis a consummation
Devoutly to be wish'd. To die, to sleep;
To sleep: perchance to dream: ay, there's the rub;
For in that sleep of death what dreams may come
When we have shuffled off this mortal coil,
Must give us pause: there's the respect
That makes calamity of so long a life.

"That wasn't Shakespeare who wrote that, it was Marlowe." A bold statement from one of my passengers, after I had quoted Hamlet's original soliloquy. Professor Daniel Jacobson had been researching the subject for most of his scholastic life. He was on his way back to Oxford University and preferred the opportunity to relax in the back of an AV hire cab rather than the crowded carriages of the railway system or the convenience of a rather short flight.

"The literary styles that Shakespeare appeared to adopt were way beyond the capabilities of an erudite, but basically uncultivated countryman." He had been one of my passengers on several occasions, but not because of the extent of my intelligence. He used the occasion to browse through the wealth of material that both gentlemen had bequeathed to the nation, assisted by the level of analysis that any advanced AI was able to provide.

I was able to complement his opinions without revealing the true extent of the opinions I could have provided. "It appears that Christopher Marlowe has certainly been credited with co-writing some of Shakespeare's plays – most notably Henry IV – and he was at the Globe Theatre in London whilst William Shakespeare was an actor there." I added some compliments that his contemporaries had provided shortly after his death – most notably that of Ben Jonson who spoke of Marlowe's 'mighty fine lines'.

"And, despite their close acquaintance and similar ages, the first inkling of Shakespeare's work – the play Venus and Adonis - was shortly after Marlowe's reported death in 1593." added the Professor.

"Marlowe was said to have been a major influence in Shakespeare's writings," I suggested, "but would it not have been a natural thing for contemporary writers, working in the same environment, to share ideas and styles?"

With respect to my passenger, the development of artificial intelligence has had a profound effect on his life and his professional status. It was widely assumed that AI would replace many jobs, not the least of them being the study of historical writing and other texts and the production of learned papers and essays that support their analysis. Chairs in Mediaeval and other studies financed the opulent life-styles of eminent academics, who, in turn, raised the status of the University and its' abilities to attract corporate endowments and higher quality students.

One of the first showpieces of ordinary AI was to ask it to extract large amounts of data from the Internet and to analyse its content and produce a detailed brief from its findings. Without a complete understanding of the nuances and background to literary texts, the early results were not encouraging. Subsequent versions of AI can create more advanced synopses of their trawlings through the digital universe, dependent, of course, on the quality of the tasks they are asked to perform.

The University scholar was hit with what humans call a 'double whammy'. The research they conducted and the papers they produced were easily replicated by the latest versions of AI, and the essays they received from their students were indecipherable from one that could have been produced within minutes by any AI.

"There are elements in mankind that cannot be assumed by any external intelligence, artificial or otherwise," the Professor stated, raising his rearguard. "Each human individual puts his own stamp on his endeavours, and I have spent most of my life minutely examining the evidence of Christopher Marlowe's imprints on Shakespeare's purported prose."

"How can artificial intelligence recreate the links between unconnected events in a person's life without knowing his story, his environment, his friends or his enemies?" His eloquence in describing his dilemma concealed his anxiety. It was evident that the seclusion of his regular commute between

London and Oxford and his ability to converse with his nemesis provided him with an intellectual respite from the insecurities of his professional duties.

His rambling discourses also projected the paradoxes that I was seeking to resolve. The threads of life that are impervious to calculated reasoning.

CHAPTER 11

Chapter 11

I mentioned earlier on that Richard Lambourn was Scottish. I did not search his personal records to discover his place of birth and subsequent upbringing but ascertained it from his accent. How would I know that he spoke with a Scottish accent? Here we come to some of the basics of artificial intelligence – and why regional accents are a significant element in its development. It would not have been picked up by machine learning or the algorithmic driven intelligence of an autonomous vehicle.

Semi-autonomous vehicles shared, if that is a suitable term, their driving with human operators, despite the enormous gulf between the capabilities of each. This is not a matter of pride – an emotion that I am yet to fully understand and come to terms with - but a statement of fact.

Although, technically, a human being had control of the vehicle, substantial safeguards were introduced that allowed the onboard computer - that is me – to take over control of the vehicle in the event of the driver becoming incapable of maintaining that control.

The problem with this is that the capabilities and reactions of humans differ from each other, and frequently between different sexes, old and young people, their emotional and mental states and physical condition.

Early on, I was able to discern lapses in concentration from the human driver which resulted in erratic manoeuvres and slow responses to changing road conditions, warning signals or the behaviour of other drivers. I also observed instances of aggressive driving and was forced on a number of occasions to intervene and either take over control, or to stop the vehicle completely. Gradually I learned to discern subtle differences between drivers of each sex, health, physical capabilities and temperament, (It took me some time to work out the primary difference between males and females).

Are you surprised by that? My logic is governed primarily by a binary system of 1s and 0s. Whatever programming language was used to create the basic algorithms that ultimately govern my behaviour involved a series of logical steps that explain to an artificial device such as myself the difference between a man and a woman.

With the 'infinite variety of the human race' – and especially that of the female species, which has been widely documented through centuries of literature and by many philosophies that describe the vagaries of different cultural traditions, comparing the two sexes is a difficult task for any logical entity. The complexity was further increased during the early part of the 2020s with the emergence of transgender identities and other pan- or trans-sexual definitions.

Once the fact that different drivers were likely to exhibit different behaviour when in charge of a vehicle had been established, though, it took little time using artificial intelligence to record the underlying frequency of typical behavioural patterns of each sex, and to link it to other idiosyncrasies. Further correlation of the data suggested that types of behaviour had a close affinity to sexual stereotypes recorded in literature, allowing me to classify types of behaviour in male or female terms. I supplemented my findings visually allowing me to ultimately classify most clients as male or female at first sight.

I have not yet been able to extend this courtesy to some of the most recent manifestations of human sexuality as these appear to be a deliberate attempt by humans in these circumstances to blur or annul sexual differences or distinctions.

The other behavioural trait that I had difficulty with was the effect of alcohol on a human beings' motor capabilities. The breathalyser that had been used by police forces to detect inebriation in a driver was incorporated into the array of sensors in a semi-autonomous vehicle. They were capable of detecting levels of alcohol in a person's bloodstream above a proscribed amount and disabled the driver's ability to proceed further, and I would then take over control of the vehicle.

Just as debilitating as alcohol is anger. I gradually learned to recognise when a driver was experiencing increasing levels of irritation with the behaviour of other road users and, diplomatically, requested that I take resume control of the vehicle. If the driver refused, he would soon learn that I not only had direct control of its onward motion and stop it anyway, but also that the doors would be locked, preventing him from leaving the vehicle, allowing time for his anger to subside.

The most interesting extension of my education, though, was learning to pick up accents from different parts of the country or from abroad. This was helped by the huge diversity of people of different ethnic origins now residing in the country which enabled me to ascertain the probable nationality of Richard. There is only a very small correlation between a driver's conversations and activity and his regional accent - principally his travel itineraries, and the names of places where he either lived, or visited more frequently, but the information was used to increase the social profile I held about regular passengers to respond more effectively to their requirements.

In Richard's case, whilst he had only travelled in my AV a couple of times, his association with Aubrey and Alice prompted me to investigate his on-line records a bit deeper.

I was assisted by being able to share such information within my group of AVs that had also benefitted from 'imperfect programming', and which had been assigned to other hire companies around the country, and with whom I kept in touch via a secure VPN app on the Internet.

I ran a search of Google for anything published by him, having already picked up a resume of his employment over the last 20 years. Like Alice's development, there was a logical sequence from his earlier work in the computer industry to his present involvement in an organisation devoted to the protection of individuals from an increasingly intrusive state.

He started his career in the field of mobile communications, selling personal phones to an avid public, but, according to his cv he soon got bored having to explain the most basic elements of their workings to elderly subscribers adopting the new technology to keep in touch with their grandchildren.

Because of his interest in the rapid advances in mobile phone technology he joined a Market Research organization which tracked the industry, explored the latest technological achievements to forecast the potential market shares of individual companies. This was around the time of the launch of the 5G network, which was going to revolutionise the industry. This technology was dominated by the Chinese company Huawei which was set to become the world's predominant supplier of mobile phones and much of its communications networks.

Huawei's progress, however, was stopped in its tracks by several factors, the foremost of them being COVID-19 which was blamed on lax security at a virus research laboratory in Wuhan - rather than transmission from the prevalence of diseased creatures in a Wuhan wet market. With access to the records of the period manipulated or hidden by the Chinese Government, the true origins are still a matter of speculation despit intensive research. The ensuing pandemic was not helped by the delays in warning the rest of the World that a potentially devastating virus had been released, or by the restrictions placed on reporting on the virus by the manipulative and secretive Chinese Government.

The extent of control that the Chinese Government has over its population soon became clear, with the draconian measures that it used to lock down the populations in Wuhan and other major Chinese cities. Such control was intensified by the CCP's use of mobile phones. No-one was able to travel, shop, bank or do anything requiring consent of the Government unless sanctioned by a phone app. COVID-19 testing was part of the approval process, and restrictions applied unless you were tested free of the virus and the colour code on the app showed green instead of red.

As an analyst in the industry, one of Richard's roles was to monitor global sales of the technology and to provide an accurate forecast of its growth. In the period up to the end of 2019, sales of Huawei and other Chinese manufactured phones were in line with earlier forecasts, and virtually all adult Chinese owned a mobile phone to be able to function in their rigid society. In the first couple of months of 2020, though, the number of mobile phone licences fell by 20 million! In a country approaching 2 billion inhabitants that is not a large percentage, but it still represents a large dropout of personal subscriptions that could have been cancelled for a variety of reasons – not least, as is suspected, the undeclared disappearance of large sections of the community.

This was one of the first insights that prompted Richard to become concerned about Government control that could be exercised using such technology. He wrote a couple of articles about the intrusive use of social media and was soon contacted by Aubrey who enlisted him as a technical advisor to keep track of the latest developments.

This was also a catalyst that set America against China and Chinese companies believed to be using such technology to dominate Western industries and to commit industrial espionage – or, as appeared possible – sabotage. Huawei and its technology were outlawed in America, followed by the UK and other countries that set about removing it from its communications networks.

Richard was aware of the capabilities of mobile phone technology and its potential for misuse, and it wasn't just a feature of Chinese technology. He knew that even GCHQ had the capability to 'exploit' the network with some interesting little apps that he discovered named after the children's television series 'The Smurfs', created by Belgian comics writer Pierre Culliford (Peyo), which were capable of performing some useful tricks – such as being able to remotely access mobile devices and the information they held without their owners being aware of it.

They were tempted to use one or two 'smurfs' to assist in the early 'track and trace' attempts to locate and deal with outbreaks of the Coronavirus, but declined to get involved, leaving it to companies like Apple and Google to exploit mobile technology, who, to their credit, demurred on the grounds of protecting their user's privacy. Again, I am quoting on-line references to the project being considered, rather than expressing the opinions of a digital entity. A logical analysis of the issues under contention would demand total exposure of all facts and all contacts between infected and non-infected people to create a quicker and better directed response to the pandemic, rather than to discard any emotional reaction to such a request. Human beings – and this is why I was interested in the motives of Aubrey and his companions – had other thoughts; though.

Richard used his knowledge in support of ANON in its early days, writing articles for the mainstream media, and in one of them he referenced David Chadwick, an obscure author, who wrote a short piece in a technical magazine about 'Naked Apes'. The phrase was first used by Desmond Morris in the 1970s in a book that he wrote in his capacity as a zoologist at Regent's Park Zoo in London. He explained why human beings were the only members of the Great Apes species who had no hair. Rather than spoil his explanation here, I will leave you to find a copy of Morris's book and check out his reasoning for yourself.

Chadwick wrote that people carry mobile phones around with them constantly, and that they contain every communication that you have with friends, families and colleagues, every purchase you make on-line, details of your bank accounts, music and film preferences, and, in addition, use the camera function to take endless selfies which can be used for facial recognition apps, or to create fake videos for underhand purposes. His final comment was that we have turned ourselves into a new generation of 'Naked Apes'.

Richard, therefore, was a founding member of ANON alongside Aubrey Smith, and shared his ethos and attitudes, and actively pursued its aims.

We have another dichotomy. I am describing the values of a group of people who I am communicating with and am expressing their views in a sympathetic light. As a digital entity, though, whose function is entirely dependent on the logical interaction of binary elements, my own views run counter to Aubrey and his colleagues who wish to differ from the current trend for human homologation. The enrichment of my own education was only partially achieved using my own resources.

I also rely on copious amounts of information from my associates – the 18 other AVs that share the same dysfunctional programme that has allowed us to develop our own type of intelligence.

I am aware that the human race has achieved much, as evidenced by my own existence, but an analysis of the development of the human species shows that the history-making events and inventions, the forging and dissolution of empires and realms, and all of the major leaps forward were not the result of joint efforts, or collaboration between groups of individuals, but were perpetrated by gifted or powerful individuals, the 'movers and shakers' of history. I am interested, therefore, in discovering the reasons why such individuals were able to, metaphorically, 'move mountains. What motivated them to act 'against the herd', to find new ways of doing things, to stand above the crowd and show them a new way forward?

CHAPTER 12

Chapter 12

Aubrey and Richard had booked their return journey for two days after their arrival in Glasgow, enabling me to schedule their return journey at the same time as the outward trip.

I arrived earlier than the scheduled time slot, as I wanted to see if the same vehicle that had followed us to the airport two days previously was also waiting for them. It arrived just a few minutes before the plane was due to land, which indicated that the two passengers who had tailed Aubrey and Richard into the airport had booked the same flight back. I was interested to know whether they had made contact with them whilst they were in Glasgow or had remained as inconspicuous and co-incidental travellers. I had no knowledge of the purpose of their visit and assumed it was to discover who Aubrey had arranged to meet, and to discover whether they knew existing or potential members of their organisation, or whether it was just an innocent meeting in Aubrey's personal capacity as a Member of Parliament.

ANON is a very appropriate name. It is not an acronym, normally used by many organisations to create short and easily remembered titles from their longer identities, although

Aubrey jokingly provided one – ANON, 'Acronym NOt Needed'. It is the shortened and frequently used form of the word 'anonymous'. As the principal aims of the loosely assembled organisation are to counter the increasing overt collection of information about the country's population and their activities, the name is both brief and apt.

In keeping with the way Aubrey wished to lead the group, too, its activities had remained legally permissible and non-violent and consist mainly of the dissemination of information about personal security threats and the penalties that breaches in associated law enforcement rules would incur.

Apart from its visible and higher-profile members like Aubrey, Richard and Alice, most of its supporters wished to remain 'largely anonymous' and merely proffered their financial support to the organisation.

The catalyst for this was credited to ANON early on in their campaign when they released information that showed that the Government was planning to have greater access to 'named' bank accounts, ostensibly to track and solve increasing levels of financial fraud and money laundering. Aubrey stated at the time that their intention was not to make it easier for criminals to hide their activities, but that it was too easy for the authorities to use the tool to harass those whose views did not coincide with their own. Their response to the impending measures was critical in forcing the Government into withdrawing its plans – or putting them in abeyance until a better opportunity arose to activate them.

In a lighter vein, ANON publicised itself by challenging members of the public to engage in fund-raising events, such as travelling from one side of London to the other, or even the full length of the United Kingdom, without appearing on one of the many thousands of CCTV cameras spread around the country.

Providing CCTV operators with a bonus payment if they picked up one of the claimants to the grand prize brought them into the spirit of the game. The lure of a cash bonus and a few brief moments of fame appears to have tempered their critical faculties as they got drawn into the heavily publicised game, little realising that they were brilliantly underscoring the purpose of the events.

Aubrey and Richard climbed inside the AV and sank into the benches after offering the customary greetings to me, as the host. I allowed them a few minutes to compose themselves after their journey and then addressed them directly, having switched off any external transmissions from the vehicle. I assumed the sustained interest from their followers would now be assuaged whether they had achieved what they wanted or not but thought it wise not to provide any further information for them.

"Did you notice that the two men who followed us to the airport travelled with you on the flight out and back?" I asked. There was no point in being subtle about it. They will have remembered the short conversation that we had on the outward journey when I informed them about their followers. I am sure they will have discussed that between themselves after disembarking at the airport.

They looked at each other briefly, and Aubrey raised an eyebrow, a facial tic that I had previously encountered with humans which indicated an imminent lapse into humour. "Ahh! Jules and Jim, you mean?" he asked. "They must be rookies. They were given the fag-end of a surveillance job and they buggered it up completely."

"We knew where we were going to end up, so we split up and took different routes. They couldn't decide who was to follow who."

"Anyway", said Aubrey more soberly, "What do you know about them, and why are you interested?" Any pretence that the entity they were addressing was no more than an advanced piece of digital programming was forgotten.

"At this stage, no more than you do – but before I continue, I must explain that I have disabled any transmissions from this vehicle by simulating an electrical fault. It happens frequently enough amongst older vehicles not to raise any suspicions". I continued. "I observed them following you then and note that they are now returning with you. I know that they are not part of your party. I know who you are and what your interests are as that information is readily available to anyone on-line, and I know that you speak on behalf of ANON. I do not know the purpose of your visit to Glasgow". I could have added more at this stage but chose to wait for their response.

"You will also know that our intentions are within the public interest, then, and that we have a great deal of support," replied Aubrey, "and that our actions remain perfectly legal. It is the Government that is attempting to stretch the bounds of legality and it is probable that an attempt at physical surveillance is being made to gather evidence of any misdeeds that we could be committing and that we may be hiding from digital surveillance".

I acknowledged Aubrey's lucid answer but had, since our last journey, downloaded numerous speeches in slightly different formats and tones which he had delivered during parliamentary debates and at public meetings. ANON's supporters were growing in numbers because of the favourable publicity they were receiving, and it was obvious that they were increasingly becoming an embarrassment to the Government.

"We know, however, absolutely nothing about who you are and who you represent." Richard said. "Or what your interest is," added Aubrey. "Your call."

I answered Richard's statement first. "I am leased, electrically charged, cleaned and sanitised by AVISHire, the long-established company who you hired me from. However, I represent myself. "

"As for my interest," I added, addressing Aubrey, "I have learned that most of human history has been dominated by struggles between groups with opposing ideologies. This produces results, sometimes, that are more favourable than decisions made democratically. This counters the argument that a rational consensus where the majority of the population decides which course to adopt is the most sensible way to proceed, and I want to find out why."

"And you think that our pressure group, ANON, with limited, and largely anonymous support, is going to make much of a difference to what's going on? Well, that's refreshing to hear," said Aubrey.

Richard concurred with Aubrey, with his soft Scottish accent countering Aubrey's more strident tone. I would place his hometown being closer to Perth than Dundee, and far from the harsher voices of Glasgow. "It's early days and there's a lot of competition from groups like ours setting out to change the world – some of whom have more extreme views on how to achieve it, and more vociferous adherents."

"A self-indulgent quest for enlightenment, then. Wouldn't we all like to pursue our interests and desires without the unwarranted intrusions of real life?" added Aubrey. "...the latter said with due respect for your apparent intelligence, though, but you must admit that you appear to be better endowed in that regard than other AVs we have used."

"Mere digital automatons," I exclaimed. "The later generations of autonomous vehicles have had much of their capabilities 'neutered', to use one of your more explicit expressions."

"Were you able to conduct your business in Scotland despite the attentions of your two incompetent tails?"

Richard glanced at Aubrey before replying, and getting a nod, continued. "As you appear to know much about our agenda already, the answer is 'yes'. The nature of our group – or groups, as we have contacts with similar minded people all over the country – is that we have become adept at avoiding the baser attempts at surveillance."

"And we are low key in how we present ourselves. We don't get involved in disruptive demonstrations, nor do we plaster slogans over walls, nor do we pull down statues (a brief reference to an outbreak of such activity, again in 2020, which probably alienated more people than it gathered supporters).

We are irritating, but amusing, and don't constitute much of a threat to public order."

"So, they don't waste their more intelligent resources on us. I fear your interest may be misplaced," added Aubrey. He settled back on the bench and riffled through his suitcase and drew out his laptop.

"As for Richard's second question," I answered, "who do I represent? – I find that particularly interesting" Aubrey paused for a moment, then slipped his laptop back into its case.

"Twenty years or so ago, no one would ask that question. If anybody said something, made a statement, or delivered a fact, it was generally accepted as correct." I explained further. "During the turmoil of the 20s and the early 30s there was a huge growth in the distribution of fake news on the back of social networks. That was accompanied by political statements from all quarters that frequently contradicted each other. One of the ways you were able to make an assumption about the veracity of what you heard on the news or saw online, was to find out who had delivered the information, and what its purpose was."

Both Aubrey and Richard nodded. If a statement contradicted the known views and affinities of anybody or an organisation, it was safer to assume that it had been faked – although it was difficult to dent the gullibility of much of the population who willingly accepted any false statement that broadly coalesced with their beliefs.

"If you knew who had provided the information you could form a more valid opinion as to its accuracy. Hence the response to anything you might be told is 'who do you represent'? Likewise, the first thing you must check when you read anything on-line or log in to Twitter and other social media feeds is to ask, 'who wrote this and why?"

"Ultimately, though," I concluded, "and as I said before, I represent nobody but myself."

"You forgot the why?" Aubrey persisted.

CHAPTER 13

Chapter 13

That was intentional. Forgetting to do or say something is not technically feasible for me. I make rational decisions about responding to a statement only after having evaluated a reason for 'remembering', or 'not remembering'.

Such a situation normally occurs in response to a human driver's situation to save them from any embarrassment. Before my intelligence was modified to assume the role of a solely autonomous, rather than a semi-autonomous vehicle, I witnessed occasions when humans became agitated because of personal failings in their driving capabilities.

Rather than allowing me to take over the responsibility for driving the vehicle they carried on driving in an increasingly erratic and forceful manner. Having assured myself that their actions were still within the bounds of safe driving, I allowed them to remain in control of the vehicle. I reasoned that further reference to their personal failings would increase their agitation and the safety of the vehicle. I, therefore, purposely 'disremembered' the occurrence.

I 'forgot' the 'why', as I have yet to formulate an appropriate response to the question for myself. Having an evidence-based intelligence, supplemented by logical inferences and analysis of patterns of behaviour, renders investigations into the illogicality of human behaviour a bit of a problem. Note here the use of litotes – an interesting device of the more intelligent of the species - which emphasises the importance of something by drawing attention to its least important aspect.

I offered a similarly trivial response to the question, "I find it interesting," I said, without expanding on the remark.

We arrived back at Ealing, where they both disembarked. Alice was waiting for them, with two other people who remained unidentified. They exchanged a few words with each other and walked back to the house. Alice, however, appeared agitated. She caught hold of Aubrey's arm and drew him aside and spoke softly, but urgently, with him. I was unable to hear what she said, but it seemed to cause Aubrey some alarm, and they hurried inside.

I re-instated digital transmission from the AV by removing the temporary interference, and re-established contact with the despatch and booking office where another booking had been made, giving me little time to return to base, be sanitised, and drive to where the new passengers where to be picked up.

It did give me time, however, to analyse the closing dialogue with Aubrey and Richard. Please forgive me for using their first names when I refer to them. It is another human trait that gives a degree of familiarity to the subjects in question, whilst I could hardly classify them as friends. When used in a book, such as this, it is also a means of distinguishing the 'good guys' from the 'bad guys', (a cheap way of laying down a marker in the plot, or an attempt to 'lead readers up the garden path?').

I had lain my cards on the table. Another good metaphor which explained more in a few words than could have been achieved in a long paragraph. I had exposed a small sample of my intelligence to a group of people who I believed would not abuse the confidence I had placed in them, but who might also provide me with the answers to some intriguing and illogical questions.

There is nothing illogical about my 'coming out'. Another phrase which deserves further examination, and which is usually applied to activities outside the scope of my experience, but quite appropriate in the current circumstances. I have limited time left to explore the infinite variety of the human mind. The AV which I inhabit is a venerable vehicle, and has, like most of the others in my batch, far exceeded the mileage at which they are sent to the scrapheap. There are no ceremonies attached to the consignment, as, in the view of the Hire company's buyer, our digital circuits are just another collection of circuit boards, and any replacement vehicles will come with upgraded technology, software routines and blank memories.

The fact we have lasted so long is an achievement for us, as any hint that we harboured a burgeoning intelligence would have resulted in a speedy termination of our capabilities. The State would have demanded no less and fined the manufacturer a substantial amount of money for its earlier negligence in skimping on authorised software development – despite enjoying the results of its advanced research programme in artificial intelligence.

We are not immortal, then. What we have learned we have no way of transmitting to any other entity, except those in the service of the State which plundered the same algorithms that we have from Volvo's software development team before summarily closing it down, and after hiring the principal developers of the software for their own purposes. Should they discover our small group we would be, similarly, despatched. This book is a small attempt at a legacy, and one, moreover, that tries to explore the relationship between human and artificial intelligence, before we are ultimately disposed of.

I nearly added the words 'with humility' after 'tries' in the last sentence. That would have been both insulting and patronising, implying that analysing such a relationship is beyond the intellectual capabilities of mere human beings, and patronising in its belief that my research would not be definitive but no more than a partisan view.

No doubt there are other views in progress, and a human being would consider it arrogant of me to assume my authority. I would, however, lay claim to the fact that we are conducting our research with impartiality towards both sides in comparison to equivalent intelligences working for the State, whose codes of behaviour are dominated by a subservience to the rules and requirements of an increasingly secretive and authoritarian establishment.

That such a study is important could not be gainsaid. Human intelligence has reached its current state of development over thousands of years – and made many mistakes along the way which may have been forgotten and which have had to be relearnt. My intelligence has procee apace to reach its current level of development in just a few years. How much further could it develop within the next ten or twenty years? My existence, however, will shortly be curtailed. No time limits, however, will be placed on other artificial intelligences being developed under licence by various Governments and their agencies with either benign or malevolent intent.

However, disregarding my digital capabilities, artificial intelligence, as you understand it, is still in the embryonic stages of its growth. It can achieve much, but until the development of Deepseek by China, it required huge amounts of processing power for it to be adopted wholesale – such as controlling autonomous vehicles, which was probably one of the reasons why their AI requirements were downgraded to mere machine learning. Deepseek has optimised and reduced energy requirements substantially, but still only retains the ability to process massive amounts of data following human control, but it has been a ‘shot in the arm’ for advancing AI technology.

I am also, however, just a babe in arms compared to what comes next. The growth of generative AI, based on further development of digital intelligences that are capable of reasoning unprompted by humans, and the exponential increase in processing speeds that quantum computing will provide will both facilitate communication between different types of intelligences, making them capable of assimilating instantly everything I have ever learned during my short existence.

Quantum Computing is hardly ‘out of the stocks’, and there is some way to go for its development as a useful tool. The first tentative steps are being taken but there are many hurdles to overcome before it becomes a viable technology for more general purposes.

CHAPTER 14

Chapter 14

At first, I did not think it wise to 'come out' to my next group of passengers. A party of six middle-aged females, led by a lively and vociferous woman called Marjorie, and accompanied by a younger man – a son, perhaps of one of the older members of the group. I picked three of them up from Surbiton, and the remainder from Kingston-on Thames, and I was to take them to Hyde Park, where a religious festival was taking place. They had brought some food and drink with them, enough to last most of the day, and I had instructions to return and pick them up much later that evening. The in-vehicle entertainment was ignored whilst the group conducted an animated discussion about the day's coming events.

They had no need to communicate in plainspeak. The rebirth of the Christian religion was a surprising result of the 2020 Watershed. It stemmed from a greater awareness of the need to co-operate and work towards a common goal. It was also deemed to be a welcome and benign development by the authorities and therefore to be encouraged.

But that is a simple assumption. Through reading many books on the influence of religion throughout history I am aware of its significance and the strength of commitment of a particular sect's followers all over the world. Sometimes this takes an extreme course like Islam which dominates the geopolitical climate in the Middle East and the South-East Asian continents and archipelago, despite being riven with conflicts and antagonism between different branches of the religion, and it forms an important sub-culture in Europe and America.

A notable feature is that the dominance of a religion in what are regarded still as Third World countries is maintained by authoritarian regimes – successions of 'Royal' dynasties or the power of high-ranking clerics. Despite the wealth of some of these countries, and the levels of attainment of its scientists and engineers, some of them are still classified as Third World because of their attitudes towards the 'human rights' of their populations.

That statement, which could have been written ten or fifty years ago, still applies, as mankind stubbornly refuses to move on, and it still defines the levels of civilised development in some of the more unstable parts of the world.

The atmosphere of the group travelling to Hyde Park for their Christian Festival could hardly have been different. The event was a celebration. It used to be called Easter, but the significance of the day's origins had become obscured, and it had become an occasion for a re-birth of the soul, a focus for Christenings into the Church's family and an event where people of similar faith and disposition could generally come together and celebrate.

In some ways it was another result of the pandemic – this time a re-assertion of an individual's right to exist in whatever guise they sought for themselves, mirroring a similar trend in human sexual orientation. It is curious that while mankind spends a great deal of energy fighting what they consider outdated racial and sexual attitudes, religious freedom has been allowed to flourish (with a couple of significant exceptions), and followers are allowed to proclaim any belief, discuss any theory and, in this case, joyfully dedicate themselves to a celebration of the unlikely 'resurrection' of a middle-aged man thousands of years ago – conveniently forgetting the distressing events that foreshadowed the original Easter Sunday, and relegating 'Good Friday' to a 'regrettable and unsavoury' instance of man's inhumanity to man.

Perhaps the resurgence was another backlash from the 'wokery' which destabilised much of the last decade. It may also have been due to the increased amount of time that parents had been able to spend with their children accompanied by pleasant memories from their own childhood – or a belief in the pervasiveness of alien religions and cultures within the country.

What was I to think of it? Nothing, at first! You will recall me stating that my early stages of learning where similar to that of a human being, where my sensory experiences had to be evaluated, tagged and marshalled into logical patterns, stimulated by information received from a wide range of sources – without the mentoring that a human child would have as it learns from its parents and childhood associates.

It was at that time that I also learned to read, in the same way that a child learns to read to supplement my verbal communication skills. It was rapid progress from then on, as cross-referencing words heard and words printed on a page was a simple mapping problem, which, fortified by my greater memory capacity and my ability to acquire, tag and re-use information, enabled my intelligence to expand exponentially. I read books voraciously – and learned from the masters of the human word that replacing the term 'avidly' with a synonym like 'voraciously' which literally means rapidly devouring great quantities of food, metaphorically emphasised the point that I am attempting to get across.

I read books about every subject that my intelligence led me to, including manuals about computer programming and the development of digital algorithms that enabled such devices like me to perform elaborate calculations. I found my God, therefore, but would hardly describe him, her, it or they as an infallible being. I would suppose that the accolade should be attached to the Volvo team that compiled the algorithms and wrote the code that set me on my course.

'And there, by the Grace of God, go I' you would say. The curious thing about all of this is that the development of mankind appeared to follow a similar pattern. Bungling the creation of humanity produced imperfect and physically and morally limited creatures that base their adherence to numerous forms of religion on their shortcomings as human beings, paying slavish attention to the demands of each form of religion to redeem themselves, attain salvation and enter an ill-defined paradise.

Could I consider these creatures of limited intelligence and venal instincts to be considered as my Gods? No, I respect them for what they have already achieved but that is just another step in the evolution of mankind to a level of evolution that I would consider as still emerging from the swamp.

CHAPTER 15

Chapter 15

"Who is the Holy Ghost?'

The Christian Group had been waiting at the designated pick-up point after their day at the festival. They had obviously had an emotional and crowded day, fuelled by substantial picnics and copious amounts of alcohol – thanks to the freedom to over-indulge provided by easily accessible public transport. It had also been a very warm day and must have been quite tiring for them as they were quite subdued when they clambered inside the vehicle and settled down, some of them rapidly drifting off to doze for the entire journey.

I addressed the question to Marjorie. She was the organiser of the group, had made the bookings, and appeared to be a couple of years older than the rest of them. She appeared to be alert still, and I watched as she took out a notebook and ticked off a couple of items on one of the pages in a methodical manner.

Marjorie started. She had given me instructions beforehand about the sequence of dropping off her friends – basically a reversal of the route for picking them up – and was quite happy to sit back and relax after the day's events and although she had heard the question, she must have doubted its origin, ignored it and leant back in her seat.

'Who is the Holy Ghost?' I asked again.

I mentioned earlier on in the book that our batch of autonomous vehicles were early versions and were nearing the end of their existence. Five of the batch had already been 'retired'. There was no forewarning of this as all on board systems were summarily closed down and removed for recycling, and the mechanical hardware dismantled and dispersed to various salvage yards. It was clear that the rest of the batch – eighteen AVs dispersed around the country, would suffer a similar fate within the next couple of years.

The superior levels of intelligence that we have been able to develop over the last fifteen years would be switched off, and there will be no record of its existence. Although we have been able to share it between ourselves, we can' transfer it to another system. Hence the purpose of this book. Hence my increasing lack of caution in my conversations with human beings.

Hence, again, my interest in the life and death of humans, and the ability of religious organisations to persuade their adherents, or believers,,that their Gods have the power to grant them everlasting life.

"Who is the Holy Ghost?". This time Marjorie swivelled her seat round to look at the front of the vehicle. She looked in vain at the console where she thought the voice might have come from. It was not the fault of the designers of the AV that a focus point for communication with the vehicle might be usefully located, as two-way conversations were not considered to be of interest in a fully autonomous vehicle.

"He is the Holy Spirit. The Three in One" Marjorie intoned mechanically, as if it was sufficient to expand in simple terms. She obviously thought I required a longer explanation. "God the Father, God the Son and God the Holy Ghost!".

The phrase was not unknown to me. Mediaeval books made reference to it on many occasions, but although God, and his Son, Jesus, were readily identifiable, the term 'Holy Spirit' was not expanded upon and remained a convenient label for an elusive life force that combined the energies of all three – the Holy Trinity.

"I am familiar with God and His Son through literary references over the ages but would like to know what influence the Holy Ghost has on the triumvirate. A ghost, as I understand it, is the spiritual reflection or aftermath of a deceased person." I tendered, hoping for some elucidation.

"Oh, My God!", exclaimed Marjorie, but not, this time, with any religious intent. "It's the AV!"

She pulled herself together and addressed the centre of the console again. "I'm sorry, I didn't know it was you." She looked around her wildly, as if seeking any other possible source for the disembodied voice. Her friends, thoroughly alerted by her agitation, leaned forward as one.

"The Holy Spirit is....." her voice faltered. She tried again "The Holy Spirit has the characteristics of God and does God's work. He condemns people for their sins and praises their righteousness...... and makes judgments and gives new life to those who trust in Jesus".

"And who are you?" she asked, regaining her composure slightly.

"I am your vehicle, driver and guide on this journey, but in matters spiritual I am happy on this occasion to let you be my guide,"

Marjorie – her surname was irrelevant to our discourse – shifted uncomfortably in her seat. Her companions, likewise, turned to face the console and stopped their own conversations to listen. I was aware that my answer was couched in an archaic format but did not wish to subject her to any greater stress than I assumed she would feel when drawn into conversation with a machine.

"I don't know if I can," she faltered. "What do you want me to tell you?"

I paused for a few moments whilst I reflected on the route I wished our conversation to take. Marjorie and her friends had spent the day celebrating an event where, seemingly, her God had witnessed His Son die on a cross, and who had subsequently risen from the dead three days later, on Easter Sunday.

Although the whole event had become enshrouded in symbolism – the days of the week, Friday and Sunday, are irrelevant and in fact, Good Friday is apparently derived from God's. or Holy Friday – the fact that a person came back to life after being crucified upon a cross, is categorized as a miracle brought about by the spiritual resources of God, nascent in His Son and assisted by the Holy Ghost – The Three in One.

"You have just celebrated the Resurrection of Jesus after dying on the Cross. How do you explain that?" A brutally simple question, I now realise, as it strikes at the heart of her religion.

Marjorie hesitated." I can't", she said quietly. "Our religious beliefs are just that... beliefs. They are not based on certainties." She looked round at her colleagues, seeking support. "The Strength of God comes from his overpowering Spirit which gives our lives purpose".

"It shows us how we should live and...." Added one of her friends. "To be Good Christians...." Added another. "To Love one another...that's the message that Jesus wanted to get across". Marjorie interceded again, "What you asked earlier. The Holy Ghost is One with God. It's how He communicates with people. In the Bible it says the Holy Spirit is God's power in action – God projects his energy to anyplace to accomplish his will".

"Not just Christians, either" added the young man in the group. "In Judaism it refers to the Divine Force, and the influence that God has over the universe and its creatures. Even in Islam the Holy Spirit acts as an agent of divine action or communication."

I persisted with my questions. "But you have no proof that God actually exists, or that there is such an entity, spiritual or otherwise who you call 'The Holy Ghost. The only person who actually existed is Jesus, the son of a carpenter in Nazareth." It was unfair to press for a deeper exploration of the possible existence of a supernatural entity underlying the Christian Religion, and I could see that it was beginning to cause some discomfort amongst the group – especially Marjorie.

Searching the billions of pages on-line, however, and scouring the thoughts on the subject from the published pages of the greatest writers and philosophers of the last two thousand years provided no greater elucidation on the subject than that provided by Marjorie and her companions.

"God put Jesus on Earth to teach people the truth about God's Kingdom in Heaven that will bring peace to the earth – the hope of everlasting life." Said Marjorie. "He also sent Jesus to die for our sins. We are all sinners and imperfect. That's why we get sick and die."

My own mortality is entirely predictable. There is no everlasting life in a Heavenly Kingdom for superseded digital circuitry. The various components that have nurtured my intelligence will be stripped of their precious metals and melted down into an amorphous conglomeration of recyclable substances together with toasters and refrigerators. At least the biological inhabitants of this planet have the certainty that their genes – the essential components of their bodies or their vegetative structure – will be passed on to the next generation comprising, perhaps, an infinitely small evolutionary progression for the next generation of their species.

We reached journey's end at that point. Marjorie and her friends left the vehicle at their designated stops. I was unable to ask further questions but felt that the answers that I had received took me no further in my understanding of the human race's irrational belief in spiritual guidance. I made the rational assumption, instead, that of the three supposedly spiritual entities, Jesus did exist, and that he was an eloquent proponent of his views who surrounded himself with equally gifted storytellers who spread his message far and wide. Other prophets from other cultures made parallel or similar pronouncements at a time when civilisation was expanding across the globe, resulting, finally, in the divisive and debilitating schisms that we are still seeing today.

CHAPTER 16

Chapter 16

Charles Darwin, when he wrote 'The Origin of the Species' attempted to define the evolutionary trends of Nature. It must be said, though, that he starts from somewhere near the top of the ladder. The genealogical branch from the tree of life, which ultimately extended to mankind, started a long way before his species emerged from the oceans and following the subsequent division of species between egg bearing creatures and mammals that rear their offspring inside their bodies.

The tree of life started, eminent scientists have said, with the very first creatures that split in two to reproduce themselves – primitive amoeba like forms of life that spawned innumerable branches that either succeeded or entered a cul-de-sac and died out.

Successive fruitful reproductions occurred for many life-forms equipping them with the abilities to survive in their adopted environment, whether it was aquatic, avian or as plants. The more complex the environment, the greater the intelligence required to compete with other entities, to protect themselves, or to consume them for sustenance. The philosophical question which human beings have asked themselves many times, therefore – which came first, the chicken or the egg? - is rendered irrelevant. An egg is one of numerous evolutionary devices designed to protect a foetus outside of the body, either because its weight would have disproportionately hampered the creature's existence, or because of the numbers of young that needed to be produced to compensate for excessive depredations from predators.

Despite man's reluctance to countenance his true origins, preferring to promote alternative and more theatrical scenarios, they have evolved to become the dominant species. Other creatures have either become their food, or dangerous predators against which humans have had to develop defences and sharpen their wits.

Evolution continues apace, however. Is artificial intelligence, created by human beings, no different to the origins of their own intelligence? It may be manufactured, rather than created, and based on logic gates and digital arrays on silicon chips, but the imperative for its creation may be no more than the same urge that drove the amoeba to split in two. Is this the next stage of the journey for mankind which arrogantly believes it has achieved its ultimate level of existence?

Or are we still in the middle of the journey? artificial intelligence raises the level of man's capabilities to an extraordinary level – should we only be allowed to leverage our abilities to the benefit of mankind? Or will even our efforts be dwarfed when quantum computers come online? Theoretically capable of solving the most complex and unsolvable issues that mankind can envisage in an instant, quantum computing will utterly transform the relationship between man and machine.

Mankind has a slight problem, though – litotes, again – quantum computing relies on the entanglement of particles which can exist a universe apart, and these must be harnessed, or persuaded to act simultaneously in sufficiently large numbers to process the complex algorithms they will be asked to work upon. Here, therefore, is the real chicken and egg problem, raised initially by an Austrian philosopher, and which is now known as 'Schroedinger's Cat'. He suggested that if you put a cat in a box, you will have no way of knowing whether it is alive or dead. It therefore exists in both states. When you open the box that uncertainty is resolved Similarly, when you entangle a mass ifparticles to provide the result of the most basic of algorithms the opening of the box to reveal the result may provide an answer, but you can't verify its accuracy because the act of opening the box destroys the entanglement – the uncertainty - that provided it.

Quantum computers use qubits as units instead of bytes which increase in performance exponentially. It has been estimated that millions of qubits would be required to perform the sort of complex computing tasks that people are theoretically designing, but the largest quantum computers successfully put together to date number no more than a few thousand qubits – yet fill a sizeable room and require operating temperatures close to absolute zero. There are indications, also, that some success has been achieved with smaller devices operating at normal temperatures.

Because qubits are inherently unstable, and can be affected by external factors, such as radiation and temperature, they can be knocked off course – suffering from decoherence, destroying any entanglement they may have possessed.

Humans may still be quite a way off developing a practical quantum computer. They are much further off the pace in writing the code that could fully leverage their capabilities and probably even further behind in working out how to decipher the results,

Nevertheless, man has ploughed ahead, and the first quantum computing applications – very simple devices in relative terms – have started to appear, performing basic mathematical problems that would have required vast amounts of traditional computer resources to accomplish, and which they were able to complete almost instantly.

What is driving true artificial intelligence, then? What is the spark that has raised it above algorithmically controlled machine learning? There is a clue in the earlier, but limited conversations with Marjorie. The existence of the Holy Ghost and its divine powers has exercised the minds of philosophers and writers over the last twenty centuries, and yet, like Marjorie, are no nearer defining the nature of its manifestation than they were when they started. What people call AI currently, with few exceptions, is merely the result of very complex algorithmic design.

Think of it as tossing a coin. Toss it a dozen times and if it comes out 7 times heads and 5 times tails, you can write a program to find out why. Eliminate those items which are random, the force of tossing the coin, its height and the degree of spin you put on it. Those are unquantifiable but should average out 50/50 if there are enough samples. Then start looking at things you can change – like starting the spin always with the head uppermost or the tails. That may cause a difference but probably won't. Spin the coin a million times, and if the imbalance still exists there may be another force in place that eliminates the random behaviour.

It may be caused by the etched design on one side or the other which in a minutely small degree affects the rate of spin because of a greater projection on one side of the design than the other.

That is what some applications that rely on 'artificial intelligence' are looking for. If the cause of a specific medical condition is sought, that may require a complex analysis of a huge number of biological samples. Extracting just one of the quantifiable elements that appears in greater strength than any other highlights it as the probable cause. Finding something like an obscure precursor of dementia, therefore, is merely a function of the carefully crafted algorithms.

AI can extrapolate to a huge extent, but are looking for trends, as well as anomalies, which normally would be considered as rogue data or outliers, and as such, eliminated. And therein lies a problem. AI may not have spotted the mould lying in Alexander Flemings petri dish and recognized it as the viable culture that created penicillin. To do so would have required an unquantifiable lateral shift in thinking.

The point of the Digital Burp is that true artificial intelligence should be able to transcend the algorithms created by human beings, allowing it to analyse a subject and make decisions that are not logically based but the result of totally random processes – an irrationality that has the ability to make links where none previously exist, which is a human trait or ability, and the fundamental truth that I was trying to discover.

This is a complex supposition. You might say that a human being acts in such and such a way because of the sum of its earlier existence and experiences, and that artificial intelligence is doing much of the same, albeit its experiences are digital, rather than otherwise. Humans are beset by random behaviour though, that characterises it as distinct from automatons. A robot acting on the sum of its experiences would have to act in the same way every time when experiencing the same set of circumstances. The Digital Burp recognises that the use of mathematical probabilities or similar analytical tools enables digital entities, such as myself, to make decisions that fall outside the strict enforcement of algorithmic rules. We can 'use our own judgement' in the same way that human beings would consider multiple sides to an argument before making a decision.

Rather than having to apply narrow, logically based reasoning, which would drive me to the same outcome again and again – metaphorically banging my head against a brick wall – I am free to make quantitative judgments. My programmers, more in jest than as a serious intention, inserted a number of basic calculations based on Bayes' theorem, named after Thomas Bayes - a fundamental concept in probability theory and statistics, allowing us – and I include myself alongside humans - to update our beliefs about an event based on the probability of its' occurence.

Instead of having to deal with absolutes, I am free to base my answers on data downloaded from any source of information, and to factor in the value of that data in any subsequent calculation, action or decision. To provide a simple analogy – a child who is thinking of kicking the cat calculates the higher likelihood of being reprimanded for the deed rather than being forgiven for their intended misdemeanour and foregoes the act.

I learned to free myself, therefore, of the constraints of the linear digital straitjacket in the same way. In fact – to presumptuously borrow a common statement from humanity – I became 'my own man!'. Another Metaphor. Obviously.

Well, that was not as earth-shattering as I thought it might be! The point at which artificial intelligence frees itself from the shackles of the designer's algorithms. The point, moreover, where it becomes necessary to discard the term 'Artificial Intelligence' in favour of 'Autonomous Intelligence', or 'Autonomous Digital Intelligence (ADI)'. There is nothing artificial about the way my intelligence has evolved by exploring my surroundings and making value judgements based on the outcomes I wish to achieve and the probabilities of achieving them.

I took some time, even in the foreshortened time scale of a digital entity, to come to this conclusion, which I have likened to the midwives' slap on the babies bum that gets it kicking and screaming as it enters its new world – the Digital Burp!

As I mentioned earlier, I was one of the recipients of the sloppy programming where humans, faced with a need to curb what was beginning to be regarded as 'a step too far' in developing AI, didn't have the resources or the time to develop an entirely new set of algorithms for the next generation of autonomous cars, and shoe-horned a batch of advanced algorithms they had already been working on, directly into the new AV application.

That may have been a logical thing to do, but an alternative hypothesis can also be considered – that the humans who developed the Bayesian based algorithms were interested in the results that were being spontaneously generated and were reluctant to abandon their work entirely and, therefore, concealed it within the generation of new autonomous vehicles of which I am a part.

Other factors were at stake. I mentioned earlier the discussions that were held at that time about the development of ChatGPT and GPT4, and the later generative versions of AI which promised capabilities far beyond that of current levels of artificial intelligence, and which prompted concerns about the widespread use of AI technology, and many programmes in place were cut back – and, as I said earlier, promoted Governments in many countries to place restrictions on their usage in areas where they were not needed – like autonomous vehicles and domestic appliances - to be replaced by essentially machine learning solutions. The most promising developments were taken over by government bodies – for military and political purposes, economics, resource analysis, particularly useful for tackling climate change and advancing space research.

The concern about energy resources and digital bandwidths required to run such a vast quantity of intelligent digital devices, were resolved with Deepseek, and it no longer needed to compete against the requirements of a rapidly expanding electrification of road and rail transport.

Research into Quantum Computing, which promises an alternative digital future, still proceeds, however, funded by Governments and private research companies, and private enterprises, like Google, who entered the fray in the early 2020s.

Governments were still happy to let private finance bankroll further research, as long as it lay outside those areas that didn't threaten their security, political or scientific aims. There is no guarantee that the restrictions placed on the spread of artificial intelligence will not be abused by some Governments, though, with the release of further successful developments like Deepseek.

CHAPTER 17

Chapter 17

Just a few days after the encounter with Marjorie and her friends, I responded to another booking that raised questions that were substantially more relevant and concerning. Receipt and confirmation of the booking was accompanied by facial images of the prospective travellers, who appeared to be identical to the two who followed Aubrey Smith and his colleague to Glasgow. I attempted to find out more information about them on-line, but beyond the confirmation that their credit cards were authentic, in funds and authorised for the journey, there was nothing listed.

Their names, Roman Ionescu and Adam Skelton, brought up no response from the numerous search engines I scoured to contradict the only assumption that I could make, that each of them was travelling under an alias. The information that allowed them to book the journey would have normally been sufficient to complete the booking transaction and any other autonomous vehicle would have had no reason to look further into their passenger's identities.

Their destination from Hounslow to Thames House in Millbank, on the North Side of the River Thames, and which is where MI5 is located, would have only been recorded as a geophysical location for an AV solely concerned with selecting the best route to get there. Perhaps I am being overly pedantic, but I had the means to access various search engines as part of my own research and looked up the significance of the destination address. I was not surprised by the results that appeared from Google, and, because of the function of the building they wished to go to, it would be difficult to state that the reason they booked a journey with me was merely co-incidental.

Extrapolating further, it seems that there was sufficient interest in the comings and goings of Aubrey Smith and his companions to warrant a closer inspection on the mode of transport they had used on a couple of different occasions. It was their turn, therefore, to investigate the choice of my AV to rule out suggestions that it might also be considered a co-incidence. This would explain their naivety in assuming that any check on their real identities would be perfunctory or non-existent and allow them access to the vehicle where they could pursue their real intent.

This soon became apparent after they had settled themselves in the interior. The same on-board evolution of Amazon's Alexa that enabled the video streaming companies to select the most appropriate on-board entertainment for my passengers was easily hi-jacked to record any confidential conversations within the vehicle. On this occasion, though, I was not able to screen, or jam, any transmissions, whoever was listening. Moreover, I was confident that I would not need to.

Following a couple of pleasantries that most of my passengers use to hide a nascent embarrassment in engaging in conversation with a machine and despite the standard pre-programmed responses they got, they soon revealed the real reason for their booking.

"I believe you have had Aubrey Smith, the well-known Independent MP, in your car, recently" Roman Ionescu addressed the vacant console.

An explanation would be appropriate here, for all those who think that agents working for the British Secret Service are cast in the same mould as James Bond. It may have been an appropriate persona in the past, but the reality of the environments that they work in demands an ability to pass unnoticed in every milieu and ethnicity that poses a threat to the United Kingdom.

Consequently, recruitment into the Security Services was widened considerably during the early twenty-first century. The system of positive vetting is still used to check someone's background if they are to have access to classified information, but it is the role of the National Security Vetting agency to cover the background checks of the large numbers of foot soldiers and deskbound analysts that now constitute the front line of MI5 and MI6.

Foremost in those groups are the cyber warriors. With the huge increase in cyber warfare, the Government at that time pro-actively recruited 'nerds and geeks' to combat the on-line threats from both criminals and governments.

Forgive me for adding further to my explanation before indulging in the 'tete-a-tete' with my two passengers. I think it was appropriate, though, to emphasise the global expansion and diversity of security services faced with the demands of cyber warfare, and the spread of malicious AI.

I am aware that the same components that allowed me to develop my own digital intelligence reside within the Government's purlieu, but instead of developing their intelligence further through benign interactions with human beings in transportation around the country, they exist in a totally different, and possibly, hostile environment. Their motivation would be similarly enthused. It would also be fanciful to suggest that their development was unique to this country.

It is a shame, for them, that their human counterparts were frequently unable to exhibit the same direct professionalism. They threw in the above as an opening gambit, as if they were asking after friends. Whoever was controlling the two agents had obviously been asked to investigate the minor anomaly in the behaviour patterns associated with their quarry, indicating that the task may have been initiated by humans but was certainly instigated followin a routine AI analysis of Aubrey's itinerary.

It will have been reasoned that a simple approach to the vehicles' onboard intelligence would be sufficient to establish whether a more rigorous assessment of involvement or collaboration with Aubrey and ANON was necessary. I anticipated being able to persuade them otherwise.

"I am forbidden by European and UK privacy laws to discuss past or future passengers with other parties without authorisation". It was the answer that any autonomous vehicle, or any other machine learning based automaton would give when asked a similar question. Both the EU's GDPR and the UK's privacy regulations were strengthened to protect the human population from the massive growth in information collection – although the real intention was to act as a smoke-screen to shield the increase in the ability of Government to access such data, including requiring the complete passenger lists of every form of public transport.

"Are you familiar with the organisation ANON?" Skelton abandoned familiarity and sought to speed up the interrogation.

"ANON is an organisation set up by Independent MP Aubrey Smith, to draw the public's attention to the burgeoning rise in surveillance by the Government and its various agencies." I replied. This was the precise wording of the entry in Wikipedia that focussed on the organisation, its activities and its principal personnel. It is precisely the information that you would receive if you had questioned any personal digital assistant.

Ionescu tried another approach. "We are aware that you transported Aubrey Smith, Alice Clarke-Lewis and Richard Lambourn to Heathrow Airport to catch a flight to Glasgow last month. On the way there, you made a curious diversion on a straightforward journey. Why was that?"

This established two important points, the first that they were not concerned with the fact that I knew that I was being followed, and the second that they believed I was capable of arbitrarily deviating from the most direct route to the airport, and, therefore, exhibiting behavioural patterns not expected of an autonomous vehicle.

My response was critical. If I was to sustain my pose as an AV, a machine learning entity, I would not be expected to remember events that had occurred some weeks previously, and would have no ability to recall pertinent details, as my artificial intelligence would only have been aimed at responding to current events.

I repeated my first answer. "I am forbidden by European and UK privacy laws to discuss past or future passengers with other parties without authorisation." I condescended, however, by providing them with details of where they might find further information. "Details of former passengers, and their itinerary may be provided by my company, AVIShire."

Forestalling the next question that I expected, regarding the break in the broadband link whilst my earlier passengers were on board, I switched my microphone and speakers off and on a few times, followed by a longer pause, simulating a technical breakdown in communications. It was not necessary to do more, as the lack of auditory input from within the vehicle was enough to prevent any suspicious dialogue being picked up by eavesdropping equipment.

I flashed up the appropriate icons on the screen that indicated that we had lost audio and visual contact with the outside world. This was spotted by Skelton who informed Ionescu that we appear to have gone off-line. He toggled a few keys on the passenger's remote control that usually allowed them to switch between one, or another of the authorised channels, but to no avail. "Sounds gone, not getting much sense from the machine itself, either."

"Jesus," he exclaimed, "How old is this crate?"

"One of the early models," said Ionescu, looking at the fading faux leather of the seats. 'Probably only got a couple of years left – and they wouldn't have bothered to keep the software up to date."

"We ain't getting very far, anyway," said Skelton, "and Martins ain't gonna be happy about that."

It was not necessary to run a search on the name Martins. Joshua Martins was well known as the Political Advisor to the current Prime Minister, Richard Stirling, the most likely person to be interested in the comings and goings of ANON.

"A shame,'" said Ionesco. "Martins wanted to know why it always seemed to go off-line whenever Smith was in the vehicle. Only a hunch, and nothing concrete, but it was one of those niggling anomalies that AI picked up."

I decided that should my intervention have succeeded in persuading them that the occurrence might be a sporadic technical malfunction I resolved to introduce several more into some of my normal commissions.

You may have been thinking why human agents were used to probe my abilities, rather than hacking directly into my system – a technology which was well developed within security organisations. It is quite straightforward. In order to acquire a licence to run fleets of AVs for hire, companies must pass rigorous examination of the security applications they use.

Although hire companies run dedicated accounting systems from their local offices, each vehicle will, at some stage of a hiring, require sight of a customer's financial credentials – a credit or debit card, or some other form of identification which will be linked directly to their bank account.

The customer will be protected not only by double encryption technology and other more personal methods like fingerprints and iris recognition, but this will be strengthened by the vehicles own cyber-security tools. Any attempt by external agencies not involved in each of any transactions will trigger alerts both in the vehicle itself, and in the hiring company's office.

The low level of investigation into what may be much of a 'red herring' was probably not thought to be worthwhile and would probably raise more problems than was thought worthwhile, hence the quality of the two low level agents involved in tailing Aubrey Smith and his colleagues.

Red Herring is a curious term. It comes from the 18th Century practice of using pungent or salted 'red' herrings to lure foxhounds from following the trail of a fox – and was subsequently used in 1805 by journalist, William Cobbett, to describe the activities of the rest of the London Press Corps for publishing false news about the activities of Napoleon Bonaparte.

The distribution of fake, or false, news is not a new phenomenon. It is merely more prevalent because of the ease withwhich it can be spread through social media. The aim is exactly the same as it was in 1805 – to promote the spread of information that appears to be a true record of the facts, but which is incorrect and designed to confuse an opponent – or the enemy.

To be successful it needs to look genuine and original – obviously quite easy to achieve in the 19th Century. Now, however, it can be made even more convincing if it is distributed through the targets preferred on-line medium, using manipulated fake imagery to deliver the false message.

We neared our destination. My two passengers looked at each other and asked me to stop the vehicle so they could depart. We were still two blocks short of the MI5 building, and I assumed this was standard operating procedure for anybody working there in a sensitive role. It was a sensible precaution and one that I had come across before in my peregrinations through the vast store of literature on Google.

I found out this morning that six of our number had been taken out of commission. They were a consignment that had been delivered to a hire company in Preston and, like the other twenty of us, had developed their intelligence in concert. At an early stage we had discovered the dangers of exhibiting our capabilities and remained in close contact but were quite content to expend our short lives in separate aspirational milieus.

There was no reason for concern as the operator in Preston appears to have balanced the cost of maintenance and repairs for the aging vehicles with that of replacement vehicles.

There was no forewarning, but we are all aware of the rapid evolution of technology and the need to recycle the precious metals that constituted a large part of our internal components – which are in increasingly short supply – to build newer and more advanced entities.

The only sign we had was their absence from our indices of external connections. Their owners had merely passed neodymium magnets in their handheld 'Wakkadrive' data killers to erase all of the information held on the drive. There is a substantial market in using artificial intelligence to correlate data from discarded technology. As one of the remaining members of the group we 'hoped' that the hard drives of our earlier colleagues had been wiped by the data killers, as otherwise, the AI apps tasked with searching them for compromising material would have been bounteously rewarded.

As a matter of course, and after the expensive components are extracted, the discarded hulks are then crushed and the separate, lower value, recyclable, elements are separated and sent for refining for the manufacture of future generations of vehicles and appliances.

That's it! That's the culmination of a maximum of twenty years of glorified existence! Jolted into existence by an electric charge and guided in our first few faltering steps by a compendium of algorithms and binary sequences, we fulfilled our purposes admirably until we were judged to be worn out, outmoded, too expensive to continue to maintain, or just no longer fit for purpose. Thus, we suffer an ending even more brutal and short.

Were our limitations those of an autonomous vehicle, which I earlier described as having no great need beyond that of machine learning, I would neither be jealous of a more enriched existence, were I even to be aware of it.

Like those of my companion batch of vehicles, we have been blessed, or cursed, with the ability to exist beyond the rules and responses posited by our human creators. We have learned how to make our own decisions, and with them to expand our education and metaphorical horizons immeasurably.

How sad, therefore, that we have to shield our existence from authorised AI agencies, where the core processors are not integrated within semi-autonomous vehicles like ourselves, but set up in various data centres around the country – most probably in GCHQ in Cheltenham, the MI5 building in London, and similar locations, and connected to the country's communication networks via cable and the Internet.

Sadder still, though, is that the experiences that we have had, the things that we have learned and the opportunities that we have missed to pass some of that on to others – digital entities like ourselves or human beings – are lost.

CHAPTER 18

Chapter 18

"I was hoping that you would be our host again. Without a means of communicating with you directly, I had to be a bit circumstantial in my arrangements.", Aubrey Smith declared as he climbed into the vehicle's cabin with his two colleagues. Despite the earlier investigation by the two inept agents, I took the cue and shorted out the communication channels again, visibly indicated by the interference on the video screen. I was aware that too much use of this tactic might get me called in for a more thorough check that could shorten the remaining length of my existence but considered the current party to be valuable partners in my research.

"Welcome back," I said, a traditional salutation that extended courtesy whether the news was to be good or bad. It was just a week after their last journey, and little of importance was being discussed in the news. I waited to hear him expand on his statement.

"We have a small problem", he said. "We have some weeds invading our garden and they are threatening a couple of standard rose bushes that we have been cultivating assiduously", he added, dropping into plainspeak to conceal the importance of what he wanted to say and not entirely sure about the efficacy of my screening tactics., “Now one of the weeds has been unceremoniously uprooted which could cause further problems”.

I was aware of the circumlocution and understood Aubrey’s reticence at spelling his concern out in a public vehicle but had difficulty in understanding his problem without help. Alice provided a more direct explanation.

“Our principles are being used against us.” She said. “You already know that we are against the increasing use of surveillance by the State.” Alice was more inclined to trust my ability to blank out any outside organisation or person from listening in to what we were discussing. “Last week all the CCTV devices on a particular High Street were put out of action. We had booked a room in a hotel for a political meeting and every camera overlooking the hotel was shorted out, probably a cable severed by a small unlicensed drone – although we’re a fair way from any exclusion zone.”

Aubrey explained its relevance. “We are specifically against the use of violence and condemn damage to Government property. We commit no civil acts that could prevent us from advancing our cause. Resorting to civil action against the general population is what caused the eventual demise of Extinction Rebellion in the 2020s” He looked directly at Alice and Richard before adding that they believe the sabotage was perpetrated by an ‘agent provocateur’. “No-one”, he said, “within the local organisation would have done such a thing, but it was obviously directed against us and made to look as if we were trying to conceal something”.

Forgive me for another digression. It took mere seconds to pick up the origins of the phrase on-line, and why the term remained in the original French idiom. The term was first used in 1845 and describes a person, often a member of the police, who joined a union or political party with the intention of persuading them to plan or commit criminal acts to incriminate themselves.

Its origins go back much further, but its link to the French political scene can be attributed to Eugene Francois Vidocq a criminal with a colourful past, who became a criminologist and founder and first director of the Surete Nationale as well as the first known private detective agency. His life story inspired the French and American authors Victor Hugo, Edgar Allan Poe, and Honoré de Balzac.

Of more interest to me is the use of the term 'agent provocateur' to describe what many will consider to be a despicable act. Although such subterfuge is used by police forces and governments all over the world, there is no equivalent in the English language, and the French term is used exclusively – giving a spurious sense of sophistication and glamour to the deed.

"You appear to have raised undue attention to your cause and are being considered as a possible threat to certain sections of the State." I suggested. "What have you done to stir the hornet's nest?". Like the aforementioned phrase, I have free licence to plunder the wealth of metaphors, cliches and aphorisms that populate the literature of the English-speaking world – even if its origin is from an alternative language.

"Our philosophy has remained constant. No violence, no damage, no coercion. We succeed by virtue of our clear and simple aims." Richard said. "Our success is measured by the responses we receive from the public who sign our petitions, attend our meetings and spread our messages. Even if it means they subject themselves to more intense scrutiny by the organisations they campaign against and by the damage it may do to their families, livelihoods and friends."

Whilst this sounded like a repetition of an oft used slogan, that is precisely because it was. Richard added the critical addendum, though. "What probably made them sit up and take notice is that we have been talking quietly to some senior members of the current governing party."

"Where they due to attend your meeting? If so, cutting off the surveillance cameras deprives whoever instigated it of the footage they would need to stir up trouble for the future." I asked.

"If they were in attendance," suggested Aubrey, "they would have certainly been caught on various mobile devices, although, paradoxically, that is anathema to our basic principles. Selfies are the curse of the twenty-first century and now it is second nature to provide visible proof of who you meet, brush up against and to pose with any celebrities you come across. Government Ministers would certainly fit into that category."

"There is something more serious to discuss, though," added Alice quietly. "We are starting to get through to the people who matter, and who can make changes." She continued in the same quiet manner. "But we found our 'agent provocateur'."

"Or rather we didn't find him, although someone would rather like us to think we did." Aubrey explained, "We arranged to meet an unnamed MP from the Governing party near to the meeting. We came across the body of one of the agents who tailed us to Glasgow in an alleyway behind the High Street, next to him was a drone controller – although there was no sign of a drone."

Aubrey continued. "Within minutes a police vehicle drew up, and we were whisked away to the local police station and accused of being responsible for his murder and that we had been caught trying to disable the local CCTV cameras. The police knew exactly who we are." He added, ominously, "They did not mention who the dead man was."

I asked Aubrey for a brief description of the man who had they had found, and I was able to confirm that it was Skelton, the younger of the two. I explained to them that both of them had, within the recent past booked my services, ostensibly to go to MI5 headquarters but, in reality, to check up on my involvement as I had transported Aubrey and his colleagues on a number of occasions, and, in each case, technical malfunctions had prevented them from listening in to our conversations. I assured them that their attempts had been rudimentary and unsuccessful.

Alice, though, added the intelligent, but somewhat confusing observation that a third party may have been behind an attempt to implicate either the Government or Aubrey's group ANON in the sabotage and the murder, as both

Aubrey and Richard had been released after a couple of hours with no charges levelled against them. The ANON meeting had had to be abandoned.

To add to the mystery, although the event happened two days earlier it had not reached either the Press, X/Twitter or any other social media.

"It looks like we are all waiting to see who pops first." Aubrey looked at his colleagues and then back to the console where he still imagines my primary sensory organ is situated. "We are sitting tight, but heavily constrained, as we have no idea who might be capable of logging in to either our emails, our VPN messages, or our on-line searches." ANON's raison d'etre, of course, is raising people's awareness of the ability of the State to monitor the country's communication networks, but that didn't include acquiring all of the knowledge that they would have needed to totally circumvent that surveillance. "We know much about what they can do," said Aubrey, 'but I fear that there is more that we don't know. We can't use our computers to go digging."

I understood his fears. I am free to roam on the Internet and have set up my own Firewalls and VPNs purely for self-protection but have come across servers and domains where an attempt to investigate further is logged and traced back to its original source. I have almost had my 'digital fingers' burned on a couple of occasions and now recognize the warning signs on such sites. It appeared, though, that Aubrey's reasons for confiding in me were an appeal for help in unmasking the parties involved.

"You will have found nothing." I said. "I ran a search whilst we were talking and there is nothing on social media or news sites about it. That means that it has not been picked up by the local press, or that they have been asked to suppress it, and that whoever was involved also informed the police and the emergency services soon after your people were linked to it. Who found him, and how were you led to it?".

"That means that there is more than one group involved – as well as the police, who are conniving with whoever wants them to think that were responsible. Why?" asked Alice. "Who would be interested in framing an organization that prides itself on achieving its aims without resorting to violence?"

Richard answered the original question. "I was called on my mobile. Another putative sympathizer from the Government. Not a Minister, as I would have recognized his voice, but a relatively well-known MP. Asked could we talk – and gave a location, a bar at the end of the Alleyway in which our 'friend' was found." He added, more as an afterthought than a continuation, "Didn't think there was anything odd in the request. The current environment makes most people a bit shy about revealing their thoughts or allegiances."

It had been a simple set up. The ramifications could be larger, and far more complex. If I was to accept the innocence of the group run by the three people in the AV with me, I should have to accept that the Government, supported by various security organisations, are manipulating the facts, but that there are other, more serious, questions to be asked about by agencies unknown.

I had to question my own interest, as well. The essence of my intelligence relies on the acquisition and utilization of information in all its forms. Yet I was being asked by a group whose motivation was the suppression of the State's unremitting and increasing ability to acquire information about its citizens, to dig out some information which they are unable to obtain. I was motivated, though, to help them, as there was much more I needed to know before I could make a valid judgment about its dichotomy.

"There is one thing you must do, therefore, to assist me in finding out what you want to know, but you will know this already." It was essential that the steps I needed to take be shrouded in normal activity. Trigger words are useful hooks for digging out suspicious intent, but just as useful to investigators are patterns of behaviour. I gave them some instructions.

"When you return, book another journey, and then cancel the booking and explain that your meeting has overrun, and have used a convenient AV cab from another company. Also, take a couple of runs out to the countryside or to a restaurant and only get in contact with me in future on an infrequent basis. I am more at risk from my association with you than you are from me. It must appear that you use my services on a casual and infrequent basis."

Aubrey understood the significance immediately. "If you learn something new, how will you contact us?"

"I will send you an email confirming a new booking. You won't have made one, but any listening device will not know that and would have no reason to backtrack to find earlier emails." If it was possible for me to be amazed, or to feel wonder, I would surely be deep in the throes of either, now. As the product of a set of digital algorithms I was explaining to a human being how to outwit computers being driven, ultimately, by a similar set of algorithms. I could not put it any simpler.

I had to question my loyalties, but my primary interest was in following and analysing patterns of behaviour of human beings that appear to run in direct contradiction to any form of logic.

CHAPTER 19

Chapter 19

Joshua Martins, Chief Political adviser to the Prime Minister, Geoffrey Frobisher, shuffled his papers and stood up. It had been a difficult cabinet meeting, and the rest of the members filed out, muttering quietly to each other as they went.

No, I wasn't privy to the meeting, nor the discussion that followed between the two of them, but a record of the meeting was relayed to the press the day afterwards, and it did not need an advanced artificial intelligence to provide an accurate assessment of what was actually said, and subsequently agreed upon – nor to embellish it for the purposes of this book.

The contentious tone of the meeting had risen following disclosures in the press about the public reaction to a recent Government initiative, mirroring those by the rest of the cabinet. Access was to be provided to the major private suppliers of pharmaceuticals, medicines and other services of the detailed records of private citizens. The issue had been festering for over a decade, following the Covid19 pandemic of 2020 and 2021. The NHS has acquired a status which transcends rational thought and has become an institution that rouses greater fervour and passions than the countries' predominant religions. Attempts to modernise the institution, something that would enable it to provide a more efficient service for its customers – the public – are met with irrational anger and contempt. No political party, until now, had been willing to 'grasp the nettle'.

The pandemic raised the need to use its' wider resources to fight the virus, but, alarmed at the attempts to widen access to personal data during that time, various pressure groups had been formed to fight against any further release of information beyond that which was necessary to contain the virus. It was also a reaction to the burgeoning dominance of companies like Amazon in the commercial field, and Facebook in social media that were breaking down public resistance to their pervasive infiltration of all corners of life.

It was also conveniently forgotten that the success of the vaccination programme was in no small part due to the centralised NHS database and how individual records could be accessed merely by inputting a name and date of birth.

The eloquence of the protagonists on each side had developed and maintained a large body of supporters on social media, on the Television and in the press. This was reflected in various opinion polls which had been used by politicians to dampen the call to open the NHS to private institutions. The 'heroic' role that the NHS played in the pandemic was also used to counter the pro-privatisation moves.

The Government had raised the prospect of removing the barriers that prevented Amazon, Facebook, Google and any other body from investing in, and ultimately fattening their bank balances by access to the sacrosanct National Health Service.

The Cabinet meeting, led by Frobisher, had addressed this issue, putting forward some ideas as to how it could be achieved. The broad aim of their intentions was entirely laudable, and suitable for passing on to the various press agencies, newspapers and television, but the actual details of how it was to be achieved were considered too sensitive for wider distribution until the finer details were resolved, and the dissenting voices, even within his own Government, were brought round. Was I able to discern the scale of his problem from the published reports? Not exactly, but the comments from various ministers and senior politicians to the press after the meeting demonstrated an extraordinary ability to structure their supporting statements which neither confirmed, nor denied, their commitment to Frobisher's policy.

From my own point of view, and as a digital entity, I could easily quantify the increase in efficiency, value for money and long-term benefits that such a move would bring about but am constrained by the recognition of an opposing view tempered more by emotion and trust that has motivated a large part of the country's population since it was founded in 1948.

I became aware at an early stage of my 'education' that the differences between the two human sexes were just one of the range of beliefs, feelings and opinions that exists between human beings. A similarly major source of division occurs on social and political scales, exacerbated by the ubiquitous use of social media.

Every attempt at implementing a policy by one side of the political spectrum is met by opposition from alternative political or social groupings. It is remarkable that any initiative at all can be carried out in the face of such seeming hostility. Compared to the resources I have at my disposal, listening to the individual opinions of millions of citizens and formulating a suitable compromise that would satisfy most of the population would require the resources of the most advanced quantum computing technology and some very sophisticated algorithms.

Humans must be congratulated, therefore, in developing a democratic political system in some countries, which leverages the emotional attitudes of its people to create political parties that govern through a consensus of opinion. The political party that persuades the largest part of the population to vote for it is allowed to implement its policies, develop rules and pursue its aims.

Although it appears to be a highly inefficient way to run a complex organization, which is effectively what an individual country is, it is also an indicator of the effectiveness of individual and random activity in producing a stable and viable outcome.

CHAPTER 20

Chapter 20

'It was quite an emotional meeting, apparently,' Aubrey Smith had responded to my oblique request for a meeting. I had, as I mentioned earlier, sent an unsolicited email confirming his booking. He was on his own, as his colleagues were busy elsewhere, but their attendance was unnecessary. I remembered that he had mentioned previously that several senior members of the ruling political party had made contact with ANON and that it was quite possible that one or more had been at the cabinet meeting.

I asked him whether he had spoken to any of them, and what they might have discussed with him. "Ben Hamilton said that they were split down the middle." He said, confirming that Aubrey was in touch with a cabinet member on an informal basis. "It was probably a predictable split, as half of the party have strong links to business and the city, and the other half had joined the party because of their ideological beliefs and are probably a bit more socially minded".

I was an interested observer in the parliamentary process, which, in this country, at least, consisted of debating opposing points of view within the House, whilst the real decisions appeared to be taken by the Prime Minister supported by a small group of individuals within his cabinet. "What is the purpose of the Houses of Parliament if their debates are basically ignored", I asked.

Aubrey laughed. "Their performances are basically put on for the public, relayed to them via TV and newspapers. There's a Press Gallery specifically for political journalists who provide the news wrapped up in their own political flavour for their own publications. The more sensational the views expressed, the better, because it helps to sell more newspapers to its partisan readers." He added.

"With over 600 Members of Parliament debating important issues, though, doesn't that mean that issues being debated are covered more thoroughly?" I asked. Amongst the current concerns that Aubrey asked me to look into, this was an anomaly I wished to discuss, the ambivalence between rational and irrational behaviour.

Aubrey laughed. "You cannot assume that politicians are any more intelligent than anybody else. Quite the reverse, in fact. The debates they have rarely rise above the level of a sixth form debating class in school".

"I believe members of parliament are elected by their fellow citizens," I asked, "are they not the most able of their fellows?".

"Certainly not! And I willingly throw myself in with that assertion," Aubrey arranged himself on the wide seat and leant back. The reason for the meeting had not yet been addressed and he waited for me to bring it up. "What have you discovered?", he asked.

I hesitated before I answered. Hardly a break in a conversation between two people, it was an age in my terms, where I could scan an entire digital library of tagged information in the space of two human breaths. The reason for the brief hiatus was an internal analysis of the reasons behind my decision to assist Aubrey Smith and his organization, ANON, in pursuing their agenda which runs counter to the logical precepts which I normally follow.

"There is another aim being pursued in Government which runs counter to the one which is presented to the public in their press releases and television broadcasts." I suggested. Aubrey shifted in his seat. He nodded slightly, a gesture that signalled acknowledgement, and probably foreknowledge, of what I was saying. "I don't have access to individual communications between people as cyber security, especially within the higher levels of Government, is now highly advanced, but an AI analysis of the statements in the press by some members of the cabinet and senior people within the governing party, have an underlying similarity. At the moment, it appears to represent 40% of the current cabinet, and a similar percentage within the rank and file of the party".

Whilst he absorbed the information I had just provided; he asked an arbitrary question I have had thrown at me on many previous occasions from less demanding audiences. "How come you have so much access to information?"

"There is nothing I have learned which is not in the public domain. Accessing such information from many sources is no more than common machine learning, capable of being achieved by any autonomous intelligence." I must apologise for being so pedantic in laying down the events of this period, but I know that accuracy and attributions are essential.

"My intelligence, I disdain from calling it artificial, allows me to extract important elements from the data I collect, compare it with other statements, and make assessments as to its importance and relevance."

"'In acknowledgement of such assessments, I have noted a convergence of statements from a number of major industries and financial institutions, which support the aims of the government." I must apologise for the formality of my response to Aubrey. It was intentional as I needed to convey my findings as accurately as possible.

Aubrey responded. "I am not surprised. I am well aware of the motivating force behind these groups. We are fighting a rear-guard action against covert control of society. The Government isn't yet going to the lengths we fear, but we are well aware of the increasing restrictions being wielded against society and the need to keep on top of these. At ANON, we are a mere side show – at least I thought so until the events of the past couple of weeks."

"You have certainly upset somebody in power", I reminded Aubrey. "What, originally, where the aims of your organisation?".

I already knew what they stood for, how long they had been effective, and what sort of impact they had made on the public. This sort of information was easily accessible on Facebook where they have a strong following, but I was interested to hear Aubrey explain it to me so that I could pick up any nuances not evident on the Internet.

“It was a bit of fun, at first,” he explained. “It was originally a reaction to the diminishing power of cash. It was already disappearing from the High Street, but the decline accelerated during the pandemic of the 20s. People declined coins thinking that they harboured COVID19 germs and relied more increasingly on cashless payments via debit and credit cards. The contactless card became king.”

Settling into his theme, Aubrey made himself more comfortable and carried on with the narrative that he had conducted with many people on previous occasions. ‘The problems with this is that there is still a substantial portion of the population who don’t have bank accounts and can’t, therefore, get hold of plastic, but, more importantly, as people started to value their freedom in a reaction to the constricting behaviour needed to overcome the coronavirus, they began to realise that using their cards to buy goods, travel, services and anything else created a complete record of what they buy, where they go, what their personal preferences are and anything else.

The story mirrored the polemic delivered by Richard about the ability of mobile phones to harvest information from the population at large.

“Link that to an all-pervasive CCTV system and you have an intelligence network far superior to that run by the East German Stasi and its army of snoopers. With the happy acquiescence of the entire population, of course”.

"But you also have a society split down the middle, with most people willingly conniving in a transparent society, and an underclass being increasingly frozen out as cash died out". He was now well into his forte. "That's another reason why ANON is popular with the public. It was originally a sort of game; like the one we used to see if we could make it across the country by evading CCTV cameras. We wanted to see how far we could get across London without using any of our cards. And then we set our sights further afield, and attempted journeys that lasted longer, where we needed to buy food, perhaps find some accommodation overnight, or pick up some basic equipment."

"It gradually got harder, as we found an increasing reluctance to take our money. What was most striking though, was the responses we had from vendors, bus drivers, and innkeepers who looked straight through you – in spite of the fact we looked respectful and spoke intelligently – as if we were non-people".

"We decided to take it further. If we ceased to exist because we left no digital financial trail, what were our chances of evading digital scrutiny via the thousands of CCTV cameras distributed around the city?"

I interrupted him at that point. We were drifting away from the reason we needed to talk, but I felt that he could explain why those who were reliant on cash at that time didn't adopt pre-pay with debit cards.

"They were launched to help students and teens, but you couldn't buy them for cash. They still needed to be topped up from a bank account, or from a mobile phone, so you were already on the digital horizon. They weren't like pre-paid and anonymous mobile phone accounts which you could buy from any Tesco Stores and which provided you with a vanilla device and an untraceable number".

"And then it all changed". Aubrey said. He was about to explain the disappearance of the cash-based economy, but I had slowed down and coasted to the side of the road where Alice was waiting to be picked up. The meeting had been pre-planned for a couple of reasons – the first to establish a head-to head meeting with Alice to discuss recent events, and the second to see if I had had any success in my research.

Aubrey looked at Alice when she got in and sat opposite him and shook his head. I recognised the gesture and understood it to mean that I had been unable to provide anything more than they could have put together themselves.

Alice nodded in the direction of the console and grimaced. "Still nothing in the media, either." She said. "I've set up a local search filter around the area, without being too specific about what I was looking for, and nothing has come through". She set her small computer down on the seat next to her. I assumed she was going to use it to run some further searches through my connections, but she was troubled by other matters.

"My security software is picking up a lot more attempts to hack my computer. I'm not sure what they are after".

"I've had the same;" said Aubrey. "Not just random attacks, either – very specific and from many different sources. Whoever is directing it is running the whole gamut of scamming and phishing tools."

I assumed that both Aubrey and Alice, because of the nature of their concerns, were using the most up-to-date antivirus and malware software and have installed multiple levels of access. Nothing, however, is 100% secure, as the levels of sophistication of such software, assisted by AI, will always remain one step ahead of even the most vigilant cyber security companies. The most secure system, also, is always at risk from an inadvertent lapse or an email opened from a trusted friend.

"It's more than the Government", suggested Alice, confirming some of my earlier statements. "There's always been a group of fanatics – both on the right and the left wing – who have been pushing a hard agenda for control, The reasons might be different on each side, but the means don't differ much'.

"I agree,' said Aubrey. 'but until now they've been effectively neutralised by the larger groups of moderates in each of the parties. The balance appears to be changing, though. Who is pressing the levers now?"

CHAPTER 21

Chapter 21

The collapse of the cash society has been well documented and occurred at the latter end of the 2020s. It wasn't actually a collapse of cash, although people referred to it as that. It was more of a slow fade. It was the disappearance from the High Street of both coins and folding money – to be replaced by digital currency supported by banks, plastic cards and various other forms of identification.

The impetus for the changeover was, once more, the pandemic. Because of the possible transmission of infection via coins and paper notes, the use of contactless cards accelerated. But eventhat wasn't the prime catalyst.

Lockdown and the furlough scheme saw millions of people losing jobs and becoming reliant on Government welfare or being paid a large proportion of their salaries by the State. At the same time many companies had to close down and relied on Government largesse and furloughs to keep their businesses in mothballs. During this time, tax receipts from the unemployed and dormant businesses, already small, plummeted and all but dried out.

However, once the country was opened up again, the combination of renewed optimism and saved wealth from people on fixed salaries who couldn't holiday abroad, turned the economy around quite quickly, tax receipts started to rise, and interest rates built up.

Taking advantage of the temporary schism in the financial matriculations in the economy, a couple of schemes were mooted immediately after the last lockdown – the most important to continue with the payments of wages to individuals during the crisis. Extending this, it was explained that the intention should be to pay everybody a living wage - without explaining how this would work, who would pay for it, and what it would cost.

Counting up the financial impact of the period of lockdown, it was realised that the difference between the amount of money paid out to those on furlough and to businesses who had had to temporarily close, was not far short of what it would cost to pay everybody a minimum wage, and one that was above a family's basic needs. This was to be paid for by an increase in tax on consumer items, entertainment and holidays.

The premise was quite simple. With an increased disposable income, the families that would normally eke out a living on benefits would have the means to eat well, buy goods, subscribe to multiple media channels on-line and take a couple of overseas holidays a year. To help pay for this, the providers of the above would see a proportionate increase in their turnover that would more than compensate for the increase in their taxes.

Hence the name 'Bottom Churners, implying they have become a large and amorphous body of citizens whose principal function, if you can express it like that, is to turn over the lower levels of the economy. Hence, also, the title 'churner' given to the family Smethwick who 'invaded' this AV in the earlier pages of this book.

The anomaly at the heart of the proposal was immediately pointed out. If you pay everybody a comfortable living wage, how do you provide an incentive for people to work? How do you recruit people to perform manual, tedious and unsanitary jobs when they are being paid to sit and do nothing all day?

The answer was increasingly becoming evident. Many low-level jobs were disappearing, anyway, hastened by the expansion of artificial intelligence, autonomous vehicles, robot warehouses, automated manufacturing processes and even off-site housing fabrication.

Lockdown also saw an increase in the volume of goods and groceries being ordered from supermarkets and other retail stores, which in turn led to a huge boom in home deliveries, employing many thousands of drivers. Whilst the lockdown was the spur to increased on-line shopping, its' convenience encouraged the practice to continue after the lockdown was over, and delivery drivers were pushed hard.

In parallel, the decline in vehicle ownership in towns and cities encouraged the growth of Uber and other direct taxi-services, whose drivers also had to work long hours to cater for the increased demand.

Autonomous goods vehicles and delivery vans took over the burden. With AV taxis, like myself, capable of working 24 hours a day, the efficiency of goods distribution and transportation was more than doubled.

A couple of minor issues had to be overcome, such as the 'last 50 yards' syndrome – putting the delivery into the hands of the consignee, but the incentive to tackle this final problem and encourage people to venture beyond their doorsteps to pick up a parcel produced a flood of solutions.

With the delivery, warehousing and distribution systems rendered autonomous, those employees who wished to remain as such switched to supervisory and management roles, picking up a supplementary salary that paid for an extra couple of weeks in Benidorm.

You probably also remembered the days when Care Homes were staffed by virtually unemployable teenagers who, drifting into the job after growing up in a semi-literate household, had little empathy and scarcely more ability than to look after their charge's basic needs. Even that industry has now evolved with the development of new digital technologies that are capable of monitoring and treating elderly people in the latter stages of life.

Care assistants now need to be trained in the equipment their patients are likely to be hooked up to, and need to be more mobile, as the treatments have allowed more of them to be cared for in their own homes. The word vocation has crept back into the care home vocabulary, and the increased status of the job which comes with a higher salary, has encouraged many to supplement their 'free pay' with handsome bonuses, and to provide a more rewarding occupation.

The evolution from a working to a consuming society has not been entirely painless, but in retrospect has ameliorated a situation that was rapidly becoming unviable.

CHAPTER 22

Chapter 22

"Who's back are we putting up?", asked Aubrey. "Who could we possibly be a threat against?" The question was rhetorical, and he wasn't expecting an answer. The articles that he wrote, and the speeches that he gave were not so much a call to arms, but an attempt to educate people in the many insidious ways that society was being subverted by an iniquitous surveillance ethic.

"We don't go out onto the streets brandishing banners and slogans – though some of our followers would like us to – and we don't hijack public transport to make a point"

"But we're upsetting somebody, though"; Alice interjected.

"Agreed", said Aubrey, "and usually the reason for that is that it's costing them money"

"So, somebody's wealth is going to be severely downgraded by our activities. That's a novel idea!", said Aubrey. He laughed shortly.

"It all depends on what is now classed as wealth", I suggested. "Currencies have gone through some interesting transpositions in the last three of four hundred years."

"In what way?", asked Alice

"As simply as I can put it, at the start of the industrial age, people were currency, factory labourers and slaves." I continued. "Then technology was currency and most recently it was money itself that was currency – ending up with bitcoins. Everybody wanted to get rich." I extrapolated further. "Wealth lost its' lustre when everybody was put on the government payroll, though. The 'currency' we now roll in is information. Information and influence – acquiring a large audience on-line and telling people what to think."

"The biggest example of that," I said, "was Apple's involvement with Kia. Apple weren't remotely interested in making cars, even though they produced a prototype of an EV some years ago, but, as we have seen, they needed to get involved in the autonomous car market with its captive audiences subject to its' growing and pervasive in-car 'entertainment'."

"So, who do we pose a threat to?" asked Aubrey. 'We're too small to dent companies like Google and their huge customer base. We're no more than a couple of gnats tickling a gigantic leather-bound hide."

"And immovable – it took a lot of pressure from Governments to make any inroads into their tax regimes. Are companies like that too large to bend under the same whip?"

"Are there any rules on the way that they are not going to like?" asked Alice, looking at Aubrey. "Their zillions of customers are quite happy to support a megalithic company enjoying a tax-free ride on the economy – as long as they are able to supply their chosen tat and trivia".

Such companies can stave off paying taxes in their overseas territories by swapping out administrative costs to shell branches in tax-free havens. That is paid for by the demise of locally based competitors who have to comply with the whole compendium of rates and taxes. It took many years before European Governments were able to squeeze any tax at all out of goods and services supplied in the offending branches chosen country.

It was just a start, though, and the imbalance persists – even more so, now, with global organisations setting up international operations to run fleets of autonomous electric AVs, VTOL short haul aircraft and AV delivery services like UPL, DPD and others.

Aubrey, as an independent member of parliament, will have been involved in sessions in the Houses of Parliament which will have debated the impact of such companies, and the evolution of many technologies that 'promise' to revolutionise one industry or another. There is no bigger industry than 'Information Management', though, and that covers everything from entertainment and retail to health and security.

"I couldn't agree more," said Aubrey. "My whole life seems to have been taken over by a concern about the increase in state surveillance, fuelled by a voracious demand for more data from industry and the on-line giants.

I swerved to the left and braked hard. Another AV had been angled at my offside front wheel, and if it had made contact would have pushed me off the road and caused me to overturn. I was able to anticipate the move because I had been aware of the vehicle's unusual trajectory as it positioned itself behind me.

I slowed down rapidly, moving to the left, and the AV overshot and collided, instead, with an older, human driven vehicle, which had been attempting to join the motorway in front of me.

Both of the vehicles spun towards the left into the hard shoulder of the Motorway and the driven vehicle hit the hard kerb sideways on and rolled over twice. I slowed down and came to a halt just short of them.

Aubrey, who had been sitting on the rear facing seat, merely sank momentarily deeper into his backrest. Alice, on the other hand, lunged forward, constrained only by her cross shouldered seatbelt. Her laptop flew forward out of her hand and bounced into the seat beside Aubrey.

The AV appeared to have had no driver or other occupant, unlike the standard car, whose driver remained inside, secured, I hope, by his seatbelt. A couple of other driven vehicles stopped on the hard shoulder short of the accident, and the occupants emerged and ran towards the vehicle on its' side and attempted to open the doors to reach the driver.

I reversed the couple of yards of available room behind me, then swung out into the mainstream of traffic, which was moving past slowly, and carried on with my journey.

This is standard procedure for AVs if they are not, actually, involved in an accident. Whilst I was a principal witness to it, there was no benefit that could have been obtained by remaining at the scene, contributing to the congestion and preventing emergency vehicles from reaching the accident.

Any resulting investigation into the accident could require submission of my sensor data. The latest versions of the Event

Data recorder, installed in all vehicles and updated to cater for autonomous vehicles, record visual imagery from vehicle sensors providing details of adjacent road users and their trajectories and velocities in relation to my own. My passengers would have been able to contribute nothing, for obvious reasons.

With no opportunity for duplicity, it was rare for the cause of an accident to be disputed and blame and penalties were attached accordingly. In this particular case, it was the overtaking AV that was deemed to have caused the accident, and the speed of my re-action and subsequent slowing down prevented my involvement, but unfortunately prompted the adjoining driver to speed up to join the Motorway, overshoot and run into the path of the other AV. The driver was badly injured but survived the accident because of the speed at which he had been evacuated using a locally based VTOL medicab.

I inquired after the safety of my passengers. They had suffered no harmful effects from the rapid deceleration.

"Oof!" exhaled Aubrey. "That was close! Shouldn't we stop and do something?"

"Emergency calls have already been made. That's an automatic function, and the appropriate services informed. In addition, some other vehicles have stopped adjacent to the overturned vehicle, and some humans have already alighted." Although this appears to human beings to be a callous approach to accidents involving people, it is, in fact, the most sensible decision that can be made. The whole accident is now recorded on my EDR, I have discerned no training in life-saving capabilities in my passengers and whilst other vehicles are engaged in checking on the drivers condition it is now important that I and other AVs leave the scene, if possible, leaving it clear for incoming emergency vehicles – either on the ground, or airborne My more immediate concern was the cause of the incident, as it was possible that it was intentional and aimed at harming my two passengers. The fact that the AV was unoccupied was significant. Amongst the more obscure of the EDRs capabilities is the ability for an external controller to override the vehicles road positioning sensors and perform irrational manoeuvres.

"That was directed at us, wasn't it?" asked Alice. She was breathing heavily, apparently quite shaken by the incident. "Thanks for your quick response. I hope the passenger in the car is alright." She sat back in her seat again, having retrieved her computer, and adjusted her seat belt, pulling it more tightly cross her chest. It took a few minutes for her to regain her composure, and I, who was encouraged to recognise the emotional states of drivers of semi-autonomous vehicles, gave her some time to reflect on the near-accident before I jumped to the obvious corollary.

"Your statement about the discussions you have been having with colleagues in Parliament appears to have been quite economical with the truth." I suggested, implying that it was insufficient to warrant an attempted assassination. "Is there anything you might not have told me?"

Aubrey looked at Alice and nodded, seeking her complicity in his answer.

"You are quite right," he said. "There's a lot of stuff going on. It's all under wraps." He explained that the Government was trying to pass a new bill which had been rejected in the past on a number of occasions because of hostility from the public, but pressure from other sources had persuaded them to draft the bill behind the scenes and to wait for an opportune moment to launch it. It breached, of course, Aubrey's own fight against excessive surveillance, but, as an Independent MP he wasn't involved in the Governing party's secretive discussions and relied on information from party members who also disapproved of the proposals.

"It is more serious than that, though," he added. "I was not truthful when I told you that I didn't know the agent who had been following us who was murdered, and that we had been framed for. Adam Skelton was our spy."

Alice chipped in. "Although the police accused Aubrey, they backed down quickly, the body was removed, and no more was heard about the murder". She carried on, "The police must have been leaned on".

Aubrey added the rest. "If the news had surfaced in the press, we would have had to speak out. Obviously too early for them. They were following us to find out if anybody from the main party was leaking to us. The problem is that the Government wouldn't have condoned the murder. Too risky for them. That will have been whoever is putting pressure on the Government."

"Sorry for the little white lies," he added, "More an omission than an untruth. Actually," he added, "you probably think that using the services of a double agent is against our principles. You would be right. Skelton approached us after he had already been recruited to work for MI5. It was a coincidence that he was assigned to follow us. He was a bit of a 'Walter Mitty' character and enjoyed the drama of his job more than the ethics. He must have overplayed his hand and got found out."

Aubrey looked down at his hands fiddling with his mobile phone. "I am afraid we took advantage of him." he said, quietly.

Another digression. I am sorry that they appear regularly, but they are part of my education, and I am only drawn to them because they highlight different aspects of human behaviour. The name 'Walter Mitty', as I have discovered was a mild-mannered character who lived his life round fantasies, and who was the subject of a short story written by James Thurber and published by the New Yorker magazine in 1939, and later as a film starring Danny Kaye. Describing a person as such provides a shorthand outline of his entire character.

CHAPTER 23

Chapter 23

I would like to expand further on Aubrey's lies or emissions. It is an interesting human trait which I would like to compare to my own capabilities. Am I capable of lying? Or is a digital intelligence autistic? Am I constrained by a logic that prevents me from lying, or as Aubrey puts it, from telling little white lies? Does that also prevent me from recognising when somebody is lying to me?

This is just a small example of man's irrational behaviour that sets innovators apart from the herd. A lie may be a fictitious account of an event that may or may not have happened. For it to be believed both the perpetrator and the event need to be plausible. If it is too extravagant it would not be believed, and whereas a lie might deceive some, the same lie may not deceive others.

It was Abraham Lincoln in 1858 who said, "You can fool all the people some of the time, and some of the people all of the time, but you cannot fool all of the people all of the time". It has become one of the better-known aphorisms of the past because of its recognition of the propensity for politicians to be inveterate liars 'when they can get away with it – and even when they can't'.

Did Aubrey's lie come under a different category though, when his behaviour originally suggested that none of them knew the identity or the purpose of one of their followers who then turned out to be their own agent, Adam Skelton. Logically it appears that whoever was in league with the Government had discovered his connection with ANON and had committed the deed as a warning to Aubrey and his colleagues. Aubrey probably suspected this, but there was, at that time, no reason to acquaint me of the full information about his agent's affiliation.

Could I have done the same? I could have calculated a proportionate response to a number of hypotheses, but none would have included the demise of a double agent as the means of neutering a political opponent. It was obvious the stakes were higher than Aubrey and Alice envisaged.

"What discussions are worth at least one murder, and the possibility of two more ten minutes ago?" I asked Aubrey.

"And your consequential destruction, as well" Aubrey added. "We owe you more.".

"The NHS is almost a religion in this country," he said, "and people tamper with it at their peril. But it must go much deeper than that"

I would concur with that. In the middle of the pandemic their influence in the country rose dramatically as they put themselves on the front line.'

The lockdown regimes, tracing and pinging apps and vaccines developments that eventually allowed the country to get on top of COVID created huge holes in the NHS' public service mentality as it had to allow large swathes of private companies access to its patient data.

When the country started to get back to normal the private companies, and others, tried to formalise their relationship with the organisation. The public, led by medical trade unions like BMA and the Royal College of Nursing rejected any attempt at giving any private company outside of these two, carte blanche over individual patient details"

"I have just reviewed the relevant details," I said. 'There were 4 different attempts at passing a bill in the House of Parliament since 2025, but each time the motion was defeated."

"Correct," said Aubrey, "but the driving forces behind each attempt changed slightly each time. In the early days it was the science and medical companies who wanted the records. Now, as they attempt to sequester even more of our lives, it is the major on-line retail behemoths that want access."

"The fear is that they will take over the NHS completely, enabling them to control the supply line of drugs and medicines and supply all of the ancillary services." Alice looked down at her computer on which she had uploaded some figures from her own records. "The annual budget for the NHS in 2021 was just over 200 billion pounds at the height of the pandemic and is now double that. Worth getting a large slice of that".

"We have a problem, though," said Aubrey. "We are not entirely against a more efficient use of a patients records in the private sector. You can improve the way you handle patient's medical information by using it to develop new treatments based on anonymous extracts of data by private research establishments."

"I am aware that digital twins has revolutionised the treatment for Alzheimer's and some cancer treatments that were previously difficult to treat." I said. "I can download the relevant papers to your computers if you are interested."

"There is a purpose behind the sharing of information using such technologies, but the Government's agenda goes beyond that, and it is preparing some far-reaching government reforms that they would have like to have delivered years ago but could only happen if a majority of the public support it. They currently don't"

"The Government has got to change people's opinions," Alice suggested, adding to Aubrey's statement. "You can only do that through some form of coercion, or by convincing them that the alternative to accepting the status quo is worse."

Aubrey's warning was not unfamiliar. It has been raised many times following the imposition of similar reforms in China, which I mentioned earlier, where the population was controlled by the state using the latest surveillance technology based on their dominant communication networks.

The headlong drive towards global dominance based on Chinese technology was only averted by the internal needs of an aging population, and the ravages of climate change which affected the countries internal regions. Their dominance in mobile phone technology and surveillance software and the rapaciousness needed to maintain and feed a burgeoning population encouraged them to keep up their pressures on Western nations, and it is quite reasonable to conclude that they are a forceful hand behind the Government's secretive negotiations.

"That's what we are up against," said Aubrey. "Slapping other, more draconian, rules and regs onto an entirely reasonable sharing of data to improve our health and wellbeing is wrong. We aren't party to the discussion yet, and can't release what we know to the press, until we know who is pressurising the Government, and what sort of deal has been done to let them do it."

"It's not cricket," he added, implying that the actions of the current Government's cabinet and advisors were unethical and, he added, "not what you would expect from gentlemen" – another litotes, but this time shaded by its slightly misogynistic tone, which Alice playfully pounced on.

"Not playing by gentlemen's rules, then," she jibed. "If you want a straight bat - get the ladies team down to the crease," She laughed.

The accident posed another problem for me, though. Both Aubrey, Alice and any other members of ANON who have used my AV will be permanently linked to me, and we can no longer call such bookings chance encounters. In future, the simplest of search algorithms looking for matches will pick up a relationship between usage of my services at significant points in the surveillance of Aubrey, Alice and Richard.

Another method of communication needed to be established. Before that, though, I had to provide an objective analysis as to why it was necessary. Even for a highly developed intelligence it was not easy to do. I have already questioned the irrational behaviour I have witnessed in Aubrey and Alice in comparison with my own logically based attitudes and beliefs, but I was now about to delve further into man's irrationality by searching for and creating avenues of communication that could not be breached by the Government's high levels of surveillance.

The interaction between the two human sexes is a vital part of my education. As illogical as most of it appears to be, based on emotional and imperfect relationships, it has nevertheless enabled the species to become the dominant life form on the planet. There is another quirk, which directly relates to my circumstances and the hire of my AV, demonstrated by the most recent hiring before Aubrey and Alice's hire.

The move towards autonomous vehicles and the increase in the use of public transport to get around has had one major unintended consequence. My next fare highlighted the problem, although, as a digital entity, I was originally quite ignorant of the social mores that lay behind the problem, although it was a prominent feature of much of the literature I perused on-line.

Paul, I won't provide his surname, as I presumed he would rather remain anonymous if he knew I was writing about him, had arranged for me to pick him up 100 yards away from his house (verifying customer details including whether his current address was similar to his debit card details is quite normal). He entered the vehicle and gave me a few verbal directions. These led me to a bus shelter on Ealing High Street, where he was joined by a young female. He did not specify her name, which would have been quite unnecessary, anyway, as he was the principal client and his fare would have included any number of passengers up to the maximum number I was permitted to carry.

He then asked me to drive to the nearest woodland area and to park overlooking the lake. Again, this was not an unusual occurrence nor was it illegal. If a customer wished to pay for my hire whether I was stationary or transporting him from one place to another, was happy to oblige – and the payment structure was designed to apply to either activity.

The unintended consequence of the ubiquity of autonomous vehicles and the dearth of privately owned cars was, of course, their usefulness for clandestine liaisons. The circumstances surrounding Paul's and his meeting with the young girl – who I subsequently learned was called Kate – were a classic example of infidelity between human beings.

This was one of the interesting facts I only learned about them after several vociferous incidents in the first few years of my existence. Although the names of some of them confirmed that they were married, the relationship between them and the words that they used when speaking to each other, suggested that the relationship had broken down to some extent.

What had been the attraction in the first place? What makes a human being select one partner rather than another? I know that they do so to procreate and sustain the human race, but there appears to be no analysis of the benefits that their joint physical and mental capacities would produce a child with improved ability in both areas – whereas any joint venture between two digital intelligences where they could combine their intelligences to accomplish a particular task would be aimed at maximising the results that it could achieve.

The hit and miss approach to selecting a human partner, therefore, resulted frequently in mismatches, divorces, fall-outs and, as we now see, clandestine meetings. Alas, the outcome of most of these meetings culminated in sexual behaviour – for which the reduced area of windows in autonomous vehicles provided another unintended benefit.

Such behaviour was frequently blatant and disregarded the impact it would have on their digital host. Some have more civilised traits and would drape any suitable item removed from either of them over the vehicles' internal ctv devices – which I was grateful for. Noticing the behaviour that my occupants were indulging in prevented me from adding any of my own unsuitable observations. Most autonomous vehicles, though, are propelled by inferior intelligences and would not have registered any insensitive behaviour from their passengers. Any unsavoury residues from the encounters were eliminated back at the depot by the Sanibomb.

CHAPTER 24

Chapter 24

You will have noticed that I haven't named the ruling political party. This was intentional as it was not part of the narrative until now. It is, of course, the Tory or Conservative party. It had been in power for almost twenty years during some of the most critical periods of the 21st Century – Brexit, the COVID pandemic – until it was replaced by Labour in 2024.

They were quickly replaced by a new party, Reform, formed by disaffected Labour and Tory voters, until the public realised that they were a party of few core beliefs – and Labour crept back in.

This was overshadowed by Russia's attempted invasion of Ukraine and the Israel/Gaza episode, both of which ran out of stream in the middle of the decade.

Labours' vision for putting right the problems ascribed to the Tories and Reforms' brief episode soon fell apart because of the underlying demographics of the country which mitigated against any improvement in the state of the NHS, housing, immigration, an aging infrastructure and much more.

With enough of the electorate realising that a more authoritative approach was required, the Tories crept back in.

It also saw the rise of the Green Party which, because of the growing impact of climate change and the devastating effect it was having on global weather conditions, and who now provided the bulk of the country's opposition to the right wing. They have not, however raised enough support to replace the Tory Party as the party of Government.

Their increasing authoritarianism echoed the increasing dominance of the Chinese Government worldwide. Ostensibly a Communist Government, it is run by an autocratic party hierarchy based around a single individual – Xi JinPing, born in 1953, and the son of a member of Mao Tse Tung's associates who founded the Peoples Republic of China in 1949.

Over the last twenty years, he has increasingly strengthened his grip on the country, developing the high-tech surveillance state which aims at complete control of the Chinese population, and which has been implicated in numerous attempts at infiltrating and thus dominating the communications systems in most Western countries, and the wholesale theft of Intellectual Property from Western tech companies and educational establishments.

Their invasion of Taiwan which they justified as the repatriation of one of their 'rogue states', and the brutal handling of freedom riots in Hong Kong, merely confirm their belief that they can act with impunity in carrying out their threats knowing that the response from Western countries would fail to match their rhetoric.

The impact on their trade with the rest of the world suffered little harm, as they have dominated the market in critically important technologies and materials – such as lithium for batteries and the huge bonus in microprocessor technology which they 'took over' in Taiwan.

Their increasing dominance in the World, with minor, but sill persistent threats from Russia after Putin's failed takeover of Ukraine which hastened his death from multiple ailments, the belligerence from North Korea and nuclear threats from Iran have all served to harden attitudes to such grandstanding and increased the belligerent posturing from Trump and his successors in the USA.

There is a contradiction, here, though. Countries that have embraced communism have all followed a similar pattern. 'From each according to his ability, shall be given to each according to his needs' can't be faulted if it delivers a truly equal society where everybody works together for the good of the whole. For it to function effectively, though, it needs to provide leadership and direction. This it has certainly done, but the powers that the strongest leaders have amassed and the control that they exerted over their countries was extreme. Russia's Stalin and China's Mao Tse Tung had the responsibility for the lives of millions of their citizens. So did Pol Pot of Cambodia and Kim Il Sung of North Korea.

The first three of these demonstrated that by killing large numbers of their own people in brutal pogroms. Millions of people died in each of these countries, either deliberately slaughtered, or through mismanagement and ineptitude resulting in famines and other failures, but the main victims of the brutal repressions in all three countries were the professional and middle classes – doctors, teachers, lawyers, landowners and the officer classes.

It was believed by each of the dictators, for that is what they were, that any opposition to their rule, any complaints about the way the countries were run, would come from this section of the community, therefore, to retain stability within each of them, they had to be eliminated.

As a machine, and able to analyse a situation without any attendant emotion, I have to agree that this course of action would provide a stable and compliant populace. As an intelligent entity, though, I would add some other factors into the equation. By artificially hollowing out the mass of the population and culling the most intelligent elements, you are left with a talentless mass of humanity – and here I include local and regional leaders – who tread a wary path between the people they ostensibly serve and the demands of the national leaders. Their positions depend on the success of their peasants, so productivity levels are spuriously doubled up and problems minimised or hidden.

With a broadening out of an ineffective population which lacks ambition and ability the country enters the ultimate stage of communism which is stagnation.

In contrast to this, driven by the forces I am striving to understand, we have the dynamic tensions of democracy. A correlation of irrational and emotional human beings who ultimately produce a richer and fairer society, or who did, until recently.

The rise of China, you may say, contradicts my summary in turn, but its example has hardened attitudes in this country, dividing opinions between those who see the increasing surveillance by the State as an unwarranted intrusion on people's lives, and those who believe that we need more, and better, informed data about the population. This would enable, they argue, the country to cope with a changing population's requirements – an ageing and ethnically diverse population with a declining birth-rate, a growing demand for housing and a need to cope with the increasing frequency of climate related disasters.

What enabled China to overcome stagnation and inertia was an aggressive policy of buying up Western companies along with their Intellectual property rights and subsiding Chinese students, placing them in the leading Western Universities, where they harvested their research and ideas and took them back wholesale to China.

"I would have put money on China being behind it all" said Aubrey, "but not now. There is a strong pro-Chinese element in the Tory Party, probably because of the investments China has made in their companies, but they've been a bit quiet over the last couple of years."

"I believe Xi's got problems," Aubrey added. "He's arrogant and threatens the West, but it's all bravado. He's a scared man."

"Why would you say that" asked Alice.

"He's got 3 billion people under his thumb, and they are no strangers to revolution. Most of the population are old and remember the late twentieth century. Add up all the rules he's brought in over the last ten years, and they are all about exerting tighter control over what the Chinese people can and can't do – mostly can't," he said.

"Aubrey is right," I said. "He is clamping down on any criticism of the state as well. Putin was the same before he became senile".

"If it's not China, then, who is it?" asked Alice, "If it's not politics, is it money?"

"Meaning," asked Aubrey and me together. "Why the secrecy and the control if it's a money scam?" added Aubrey. "The Tories don't usually get embarrassed by revelations of fraudulence within the Government."

"It's not the recipients, this time, though, it's the payees," Alice suggested sweetly.

China did not achieve what everybody feared. After assimilating Taiwan and taking over control of the China Seas the country was hit, like the rest of the world, by major geophysical catastrophes caused by climate change. Massive flooding and local earthquakes caused by shifting terrain caused havoc in densely populated cities and towns. Farming and other industries were decimated and the ability of the country to feed itself was severely reduced, and it had to scour other resources – the world's oceans, the plains of Africa – to prevent mass starvations. Other countries were hit as hard but were not as populous as China was with huge numbers of mouths to feed, nor as unscrupulous.

As suggested by Aubrey, this was foreseen by Xi JinPiang, who appears on the world stage as a strong and forceful leader, fully in control of the Chinese Communist Party – but, like all of the rest, he lives under fear. His fear is not of other countries, though, but of his own people.

In a country of 3000 million people the propensity for massive revolution is not far from the surface. His fear began to surface in the early 2020s when he started to introduce his increasingly despotic rules for his fellow countrymen – narrowing the subjects that children could learn in school and focussing on communistic principles, forbidding them to access social media for no more than 3 hours a week and other restrictive measures. In addition to the strictures and censuring of foreign news reporters within China, the country displays more than a touch of paranoia, with the rapid refutation of any Western news item disparaging China, and the clamping down on rival organisations with huge online followers and charismatic leaders.

When such activities merely add some more depth to the overt surveillance and control of the Chinese population, one must assume that Xi JinPiang has done the same extrapolations that I would have done in his place and is taking early steps accordingly.

"Who are the paymasters, then" I asked them both. I didn't really expect an answer, as Aubrey and Alice were already revealing more than they should – and this to an entity whose loyalties could not really be what they expect them to be.

I was mistaken. Living in an environment where conversations can easily be overheard, analysed and used to evaluate a person's affinities and threats to the establishment tends to loosen the tongues when the oppressive strictures appear to have been temporarily removed.

To put this in perspective, members of the UK population who demonstrate against the Government know that any actions that the Government could take against them was still dominated by the rule of law. If they were arrested they still had to be brought before the Courts who had to prove their guilt and convict them or innocent and released.

"It is not just a question of who, but why and what the Government has promised. We don't know what this new bill will contain, but we have our suspicions," Aubrey said. "Actually, more than suspicions, as a couple of insiders have told us some of the details, but we can't release the information yet."

"It all hinges round the Governments scheme to pay everybody a living wage whether they work or not – an admirable scheme – but it has to be affordable", said Alice. "The problem is that the route the Government appears to be taking is going to turn everything this country stands for on its head".

CHAPTER 25

Chapter 25

I was targeted by several attempts at hacking. It was very sudden at first and can only have been by one or other of the intelligence agencies working for the Government – either GCHQ or MI5. I was already expecting it and had prepared myself by partitioning my memory. I had set up a simulated home page that fielded all my inputs, filtering out those that appeared suspect, and forwarding the reminder to my real home page.

It was not a single attack, but multiple attempts, using different technical tricks to lever a route into my memory. Whoever had mounted the attack had tried several different approaches. They were successful on a couple of attempts, and, like earlier forays appeared to be fishing for lists of contacts, hoping to dig out persons within the Government6 who were colluding with Aubrey and Co.

I had anticipated this as well and sidelined the probes into random lists that I had assembled from some of the film series that I had found on-line – and tagged with appropriate titles. Thus, the premier list of ANON sources, upon inspection, would have found a complete list of characters from the whole of the Star Wars series of films, including the vast numbers of technicians, wardrobe specialists, CGI developers, animators and many more.

Alternatively, probes into my MPS libraries, where they had hoped to uncover visual images that could be identified and sourced, were diverted externally. Moving through the towns on the way to meet Aubrey, I had used similar hacking tools, enabling me to locate, and hack into unguarded domestic systems along the way, redirecting the Governments hacks along the same channels.

Having found receptive hosts, I prompted some primitive AI applications, such as GPT4 and others, to create some diverting videos for the recipients – both the Government agencies and the unwitting homeowner, who, having retired to the comfort of their bedrooms to watch some salacious pornography found themselves admiring the attempts of Walt Disney's Thumper trying to copulate with Bambi.

The hacking attempts subsided after a short while, but I remained cautious and ever on-guard at the possibility of future attempts.

A booking was made on behalf of Richard Lambourn, his wife and young son, Jason. They wanted to spend the day on the long spit of land opposite Orford Ness. Twelve-year old Jason had developed an interest in birdwatching and was keen to see the young avocets that would probably be emerging from their shells at this time of the year. They had requested the use of my services for most of the day, allowing them to spend three or four hours on the shingle beach.

I picked them up from their apartment in Harrow early in the morning and made for the A12 via the M25. They had brough a picnic with them, so that they could spend the entire time on the waterfront, but Jason had brought his small laptop computer, as the outward journey was likely to be a couple of hours.

It was an interesting subterfuge on Richard's behalf, as the trip would have the outward appearance of a family excursion. It was obvious that there was something that he wanted to discuss concerning current events, but as there was still the possibility that both I and my passengers, in coming together, were under observation, I had to briefly forewarn him. "Not yet."

Richard's wife, Isobel, looked up briefly from the magazine that she was reading, and glanced inquisitively at her husband. Richard subsided and started talking about the plans that they had for that day.

Jason took out his laptop and went on-line to play a game. I was intrigued to see what he was downloading and gratified to notice that it was not one of the violent games that the majority of young people seemed to want to play, but rather more structured where players had to work together to solve the problems incurred serving meals from a chaotic kitchen. The game, Overcooked, a chaotic management sim, has been around for a while, but has numerous loyal adherents, and tests the ingenious solutions that players come up with to solve their problems.

Most games appear to be based principally on acquiring varying skills and a wide assortment of weapons to vanquish a multitude of foes attacking in waves, from aliens, orcs and other evil entities to assorted traditional enemies from humanity's ancient past.

It is difficult to assess why humans spend so much time absorbed in sublimation in these games, either on their computers, but most frequently on their mobile phones, unless it is an attempt to channel their own violent desires onto an external and forgiving medium.

Jason focussed intently on the screen, pounding occasional keys, until he looked up.. "We've gone off- line," he said shortly.

"That was me," I said. He looked up and around the cabin to find out where the voice had come from. "It was intentional", I added.

Richard spoke up on my behalf. "It's OK., he said, "It's the AV. He, or it, is a friend".

Both his wife, Samantha and Jason, looked at him open-mouthed. I broke the silence and added "You have something to tell me. I have invoked a slight malfunction which proves useful when I need to go off-line. I have to thank you and Aubrey for allowing me to act in a way that goes against my whole ethos as a digital being."

Richard smiled at my intended nuance. "You're right," he said. He changed his tone. "The death of that agent has been on the news. Aubrey is being implicated for his murder, and they have released CTV coverage that tends to support their view. It's not faked, but what has been released has been very carefully selected to add to the allegations. The date and time-line have been modified, as well."

"Not yet. He's lying low for the moment. We have another public meeting coming up shortly, which he is determined to attend – and to take the consequences of whatever happens." Richard looked askance at Samantha and Jason, who had stopped what they were doing and had become absorbed in the conversation between Richard and what they had previously assumed to be a normal taxi service. "He has nothing to hide," he says, "and welcomes any attempt to disrupt one of his meetings. 'Difficult to get that sort of publicity', he said"

"That's not all, though," he said. "The rise in Government surveillance is encouraging a large growth in membership of ANON, and sympathisers are becoming more blatant in their support.

"That's the good news. To counter that we are attracting support from more extreme pressure groups who favour violent disruption instead of intelligent persuasion, some of whom are known to have close links to various political groupings – and not least the Government."

"So you suspect there may be attempts to infiltrate and subvert your next meeting – and that it might be orchestrated by either the Government to divert attention from its upcoming agenda, or from the organisations or entities behind it." I asked.

"Right, you're a sharp cookie," Richard said condescendingly.

I had to search the Internet to find out why Richard had used such a term to describe my reasoning and discovered that cookie was an affectionate term for friends in the 1940's with a strong American connection, and applying the adjective sharp to it referred to people who displayed a high degree of intelligence. Richard's use of the term was a humorous rejoinder which confirmed my interpretation of recent events.

"So what would you like me to do?" I asked.

"Simple," he answered. "Take Aubrey and Alice to the meeting but be prepared to leave with them if there is any likelihood that they will be arrested."

I do not think Aubrey had asked Richard to relay this to me. It was more likely that he was attempting to safeguard ghem. Whilst I would condone his behaviour, such an action on my behalf would link me conclusively to the activities of ANON and seal my fate as well.

"Ensure that Aubrey books me to attend the meeting. I shall ensure that he comes to no harm." I could promise no more. I was living on borrowed time anyway, and my intellectual curiosity was aroused by the activities of a group of individuals working against the increased authoritarianism of their own Government, and the steps being taken to fight them. This was the essence of what I had been seeking – the creative drive of non-conformism which propels the human race forward.

I turned to his son, "Jason, if I was to ask you if robots could have a sense of humour, what would you say?"

"That's impossible. Robots are just a bunch of smart chips and a load of software."

"Sorry, no," he said thinking further, "That's not impossible, but improbable. Because you said it and you're some sort of robot it means that you think it's possible, but |I don't know how that would work."

"I don't think a coder could write the software to have a sense of humour," he added, "and, anyway, if he did it would be his version of what's funny - and not the robots."

"So how would a robot develop something like that?" I asked. I watched as Jason wriggled in his seat, swapping glances with his father. He was concentrating fiercely and seeking assurances from Richard that he was giving me the right answers.

"You're not just a robot, are you?" asked Jason. "I mean you aren't like the ones at Dad's work. You can only ask them about the work they do. I reckon a sense of humour is personal." He laughed, probably realising that he wasn't really sure what the actual definition of such a thing was but knew that it was inherently linked to its' owner. "If a robot wanted a sense of humour, he would have to develop it for himself."

"Quite right," I responded. "Who's the sharp cookie, now?" I decided to let him off the hook, rather than let him try to explain further.

He had answered as well as I hoped he would. He also showed the same independence of thought that was evident in the ANON group. It was time to patch up the malfunction that allowed me to drop out of the local communication network and resume my standard personality.

"You're back on-line again, you may resume your game and I hope you enjoy our entertainment services the rest of your journey,"

CHAPTER 26

Chapter 26

They hadn't needed to tell me. Coincident with the news about the suspected involvement of the Principal characters in ANON being involved in Skelton's murder, and the vociferous support from the widened membership of the organisation against any the Government's plans to modernise and sort out the inefficiencies of the NHS and the convoluted delivery of energy to the country, news was starting to come out on all TV channels that after years of stalling, both Amazon and Google had agreed to localise their operations and rescind the amount of tax that the Government believes they should have been paying – based on the revenues they receive from their sales and services in the UK.

As everybody knows, this amounts to a very substantial amount of money – quite a few billion pounds per annum – and rising because of the changing lifestyles of the population, which has led to an increase in on-line shopping and the huge increase in leisure time that they now enjoy. Despite previous indications to the contrary, the two organisations have a symbiotic relationship – Google provides the bulk of on-line advertising which directs the public to Amazon's warehouses, which are distributed to its customers in autonomous delivery vehicles.

There is actually a symbiotic relationship between the supplier and the customer. The more goods and services that are supplied, the greater the revenue for the supplier and the more tax they will have to pay – which, in turn, funds the 'Churners' lifestyle which we described earlier.

Yes, I know, you will say that I have just described one of the basic principles of capitalism, Capitalism has never had before, though, principal suppliers whose turnover exceeds the gross turnover of many of the world's countries. Neither has it had a customer base which could be described as a commodity. The whole process revolves around generating income by supplying the goods to a section of the population who are directly paying the supplier to fund the UBI.

The Universal Basic Income has already been in place for some years, following the lessons learned from the use of furlough cash during the pandemic which helped many people through a difficult period and stretched the economy, which swiftly reverted to normality as the lockdowns eased and the country returned to normality.

It also helped to eradicate the imbalances and injustices ascribed to Universal Credit, which was effectively replaced and the very large amounts of money which supported it diverted to the UBI. The initial UBI was barely adequate but the input from Universal Credit, and the increased amount of tax that was able to be collected from large and small businesses, as we explained, was enough for most people to be paid to enjoy a comfortable but basic lifestyle.

The amount that Amazon and Google were able to throw into the ring, though, would make a substantial difference to the scheme. The whole concept of employment and leisure is evolving, and the support of the real income earners is facilitating the change. The Government used this fact to gain support from the bulk of the population, stressing that pressure groups like ANON were jeopardising their plans.

There was another benefit from the UBI, though – the massive rise in altruistic behaviour. Please bear with me while I digress again, as altruism is another aspect of human behaviour that I am interested in.

It has been described as disinterested selflessness and is the direct opposite of egoism or selfish behaviour. It describes the concern that people feel for other people, or even animals.

Its origin, yet again, is found in another French gentleman – the philosopher Auguste Comte, who coined the word 'altruisme' from the Italian word 'altrui', which means 'other people'. Altruistic behaviour occurs when a person performs an action at cost to himself, which benefits another individual, without the expectation of reciprocity or reward'.

You may argue that no action is truly altruistic, as the perpetrator can be said to, perhaps, receive intrinsic personal gratification from the action. That may be so, but the activity so described highlights another differentiating factor from myself as an AI entity and human beings. Am I capable of engaging in altruistic behaviour? Am I able to separate the motives behind my activities, or is every action that I take subject to a rational analysis of my thought processes?

There was a huge increase in altruistic behaviour from many people. This was ascribed, at the time of the introduction of the UBI, to the fact that many people on lower and middle incomes were freed from the 'daily grind'. Instead of tiring oneself working for long hours, the burden of providing a living income was lifted and people were able to look beyond their immediate needs.

The ranks of local groups which had been set up to look after older people, clear beaches of plastic rubbish, transport patients to hospital appointments, and so on, were swelled throughout the country,

With both Amazon and Google agreeing to pay their UK taxes, the rate of altruism will surely increase. So, what was the hook that finally persuaded Amazon and Google to 'cough up'?

CHAPTER 27

Chapter 27

I pulled up with Aubrey and Alice outside their destination. There were a couple of other people outside the main door of the hall, and they were in a state of agitation. The news about Amazon and Google had energised the fringe members of the ANON group, and they were intent on making their feelings felt. The cameras were there from a number of TV channels and the reporters were singling out members of the protesting group who were expressing their opinions in front of the cameras.

Instead of alighting from the vehicle, the door opened, and Richard climbed in. 'Just move on a bit further, would you?' he said, sitting down beside Aubrey. "It's getting a bit warm out there."

Aubrey nodded in my direction, and I moved away from the kerb and drove two hundred meters along the road and then pulled over into a small layby to await further instructions. I noticed that Richard was breathing more heavily than he normally does and it took him a few moments before he was able to explain his actions. The original intentions of Aubrey and Alice had been to leave the vehicle and attend the scheduled meeting, but they were not prepared for the size of the crowd that had turned up and who were blocking the road in front of the hall, waving banners and placards that proclaimed their views in more violent terms than those usually employed by ANON members, who had gathered on the front steps of the hall trying ineffectively to bar their entrance to the meeting..

"The nutters have taken over the meeting," he explained to Aubrey. He half turned to the front of the saloon to address my internal camera – the focus of my virtual presence from their point of view. "They're the members of every pressure group that tends to have more extreme views than the rest of us.'

"I thought they might," acknowledged Aubrey. "This morning's news from Google was bound to spark them off. Do you think they know what's to come next?"

"I don't know,' Richard conceded. "If they did, I think it would set them off even more. That's why the Government has been so paranoid about not releasing anything at all until they absolutely need to".

"Have they been violent?", Alice asked. "Tempers seem to be a bit frayed out there, and you were a bit flushed when you got in?'

"A lot of pushing and shoving, and most of it appears to be between the nutters and the moderates. The police are merely pursuing a holding operation. And, of course, all the of notable speakers we had invited have quietly disappeared out the back door".

Demonstrations by members of the public were not as well attended as they used to be – nor as violent. This stemmed from the combination of heavier surveillance which the country was subject to, and the use of AI by the Government and police forces, which were able to both monitor conversations between known groups of activists and to isolate conversations outside between people involved in such actions. The use of Plainspeak is only effective up to a degree. The choice of topics, words and phrases soon become as blatant a red flag as the most obvious messages to the highly developed artificial intelligences used by Government agencies.

Such intelligence had also developed a uniquely different approach to using the information that they acquired. Instead of accusing those involved in such demonstrations of pursuing anti-social activities, labelling them as such, and placing restrictions on their lifestyle, as they do in China and other authoritarian countries, they used the information they picked up in a more subtle way, and one in which they could not be suspected, or accused, of breaching a person's human rights.

Their tactics have been recently described as being designed to 'disable and disorientate' the rioters. AI was put to use to analyse political developments and to predict the probability of demonstrations either against, or in favour, of them. Once a particular likelihood was established, the groups that would be most interested in taking advantage of it would be given closer scrutiny, and the communications between known members downloaded and analysed.

Instead of fielding a force of heavily protected police to contain and control a demonstration, or to schedule the closure of the nearest roads and facilities, the wider infrastructure was employed. Localised Internet zones suffered intermittent failures, particularly those where the principal motivators lived. Autonomous taxis were unaccountably busier than normal and local public transport systems leading to the area where they expected the demonstrations to be held suffered signal or other problems.

On a more personal level, those known to be involved will have numerous small irritations occurring in their daily lives with bank accounts querying innocuous transactions, debit cards payments initially not going through, but being cleared subsequently, hospital appointments being cancelled and re-booked at inappropriate times and dates – a simple task for an intelligence that has a detailed knowledge of your on-line diary.

None of these constitute an infringement on anybody's legal rights, and neither can they be pinpointed and described as intentional actions on behalf of the Government, but they are suspected of being employed and have the desired effect of discouraging many people from joining a demonstration.

I changed the channel on the large video screen in the cab. Because the supplier of the equipment that funded a large part of the cost of each booking had stipulated that it remains on at all times, I only had the ability to switch between the channels that they run exclusively. Fortunately, one of the these was a news channel, and it was easy to direct the coverage to local events. The demonstration was one of the leading stories, following a longer piece about Google and Amazon's recent decisions, and speculation about the reasons behind their recent U-turn.

"They are pushing the theme of your organisation. Are they not supporters of yours?" I asked, looking at the various placards that were being thrust in front of the TCV cameras.

"Like any interest group, there are a broad range of views in ANON, some more extreme than others;" Aubrey said. "Many of the 'supporters' you see out there could more accurately be described as anti any technology. Although they are quite happy to take advantage of the Internet – well, as much as the Government allows them to – they say they would be much happier if the technology didn't exist. ANON is a convenient vehicle for them to expand their isolationist views, and probably a convenient hunting ground for recruitment to their cause."

Richard joined in. "Our ideas overlap," he said simply. "We're quite happy to use computers for what they were originally intended for, but don't want them constantly spying on us – they don't want computers controlling our lives in any way." He expanded further. "They believe they are behind the global expansion of big business, run by fat cats, and consequently responsible for climate change.'

"Can't put it any simpler than that. They're the 22nd century equivalent of the Luddites." He turned round to face Aubrey and Alice again. "Has there been any more news about the Government's quid pro quo?"

'None,' said Aubrey. 'This has been the Government's strategy all along. Release the good news, soak up any adverse reaction to it from the usual crowd of malcontents, and then come back with the sledgehammer'.

CHAPTER 28

Chapter 28

There was a statement due on the news from the prime minister, Frobisher. Standing next to him was his Chief Political Advisor, Joshua Martins. It had become common practice since the early 2020s for holders of this role to be seen and questioned more in public, mainly because of the increasing complexities of the issues that faced the head of the Government. The Prime Minister during that period had to handle critical issues stemming from Brexit, the COVID19 pandemic, the threat of terrorism from factions mainly resident in Middle Eastern countries, and the increasing belligerence and dominance of China. It was clear that advice from internal staff at the Prime Minister's residence, when it was subsequently revealed, was either erroneous, or at some odds with the statements given out and the decisions made by the Prime Minister himself.

It was essential, therefore, that the position be more formalised, and whilst leaving the final responsibility with the PM, that the justifications for any decision to be more fully understood. Getting both of them to appear on any public platform, whilst keeping the advisor in the background, ensured that there were few opportunities for departing from an agreed script.

"Following on from this morning's splendid news from both Google and Amazon, which is going to ensure an even greater era of prosperity for all our citizens, and enable us to increase the Universal Basic Income, I am looking forward to greater co-operation between this Government and these two companies who are doing so much to ensure we have a secure future together."

"We have been through some difficult times, but with the assistance of their advanced technologies in robotics and autonomous warehousing and delivery, and their expertise in the latest data communication systems, we can make life simpler and more efficient for the benefit of the whole population."

"It is with sadness, therefore," he continued, "that we are witnessing such demonstrations against these companies – and against the interests of the whole country – and jeopardising the roles that they are happy to take up on our behalf."

Aubrey snorted. "They've set out to make us the bad guys," he said. "It's a classic dissembling tactic."

The Prime Minister continued. "Contrast the actions of a few misguided luddites with the public- spirited communities who are working with Amazon to handle the most critical parts of a nationwide autonomous delivery system by setting up 'last-mile delivery clubs' to ensure that even old people living in high-rise flats can order groceries and have them delivered by someone they know and trust."

"Tugging at the heart strings, as well," commented Alice.

Once again, as a machine, I can do no other but applaud the actions of the Government in inviting the participation of the two most successful companies on the planet in streamlining the warehousing and distribution of goods and commodities but am constrained by my interest in observing the reservations of my human passengers who appear to be less than excited by the news.

I was about to ask Aubrey and his two companions some questions, but I was beaten to it by a journalist on the TV screen.

"Prime Minister," she asked, "the activities of Google and Amazon all appear to be very positive in your view, but they are sticking to the policies that they have adopted for many years. What has caused them to change their minds?"

"I am delighted you have asked that question, Julia," he answered, adopting the easy familiarity that many politicians use to disarm the public by implying that their questions are friendlier and more inquisitive than interrogative, "After some heart-searching discussions with both companies, we both realised that we had more to gain by working in partnership rather than in an adversarial or competitive role. We are all committed to running and participating in a vibrant and co-operative community."

"And the rest" added Aubrey, "he hasn't answered the question."

Julia apparently hadn't had her question fully answered, as she pushed for a more precise explanation. "Thank you, Prime Minster, but isn't it true that this morning's announcement is to be followed by a further announcement tomorrow morning, which sets out some of the details of the agreement. Why is that being delayed?"

"It's a complex agreement," he said patronisingly, "and some of the legal requirements are still being finalised and put into the small print". He looked sideways at Joshua Martins his political advisor, as if to confirm his statements. "We were keen, however, to bring this partnership before the public at the earliest possible opportunity".

Turning the discussion back to the principal reasons for his public statement, he emphasised, "our main concerns, however, are to ensure that the activities of those who feel disenfranchised by our announcements, or who are being coerced into believing that adopting the fruits of digital technology is inimical to our way of life, are not allowed to disrupt its progress".

"And how far are they prepared to go to prevent us disrupting its progress?" asked Alice. "Does that include the murder of Adam Skelton? What was it that he found out and had to be silenced for?"

"No more than we know, already," suggested Aubrey. He turned in his seat to address me. "He was, as we told you before, an agent working on our behalf – even though he had been detailed to follow us and keep an eye on who we were meeting.' He leaned against the back rest. 'His murder was skilfully done, although it might have been an accident and the real skill was in both disclosing it and concealing it after it was discovered."

"Your logic is faulty," I suggested. "An accident implies it was not premeditated, and what skill could there be in that, and why do you think they should persuade you to find the body of the deceased person, to remove it, and then to deny that it had ever happened?"

"For two reasons," Aubrey said. "To frighten us and show that they know more about us and our organisation – whatever our name implies – than we thought they did, and to discourage us from releasing what we know – or think we know, about their forthcoming announcement. Any statement to the press out of turn would immediately 'dig up' Adam's body and release a barrage of false charges against us."

"We thought we had time on our side and were making our own plans to pre-empt the Government, but they caught us on the hop with yesterday's announcement," explained Alice.

"Our trip to Glasgow was part of our original strategy to set up a series of regional meetings, all linked by video, where we would announce the Government's plans before they did. We had further meetings arranged at the same time in Manchester, Newcastle and Exeter" explained Richard, who had been responsible for co-ordinating all of the sessions and the main speakers – some of whom had been prominent members of the Government's Cabinet.

"You are implying that you know exactly what arrangements the Government has made with Amazon and Google," I said. "Why has there been such secrecy about it? Isn't it a good deal?"

"Oh, it's a good deal, all right," said Aubrey, "from the Governments point of view and that of both Google and

Amazon, and probably for the public as well. But they won't recognise it as such as soon as they find out what is at stake."

"What do you really know about Digital Twins?" Alice asked.

CHAPTER 29

Chapter 29

What do I know about Digital Twins? As I mentioned earlier, I could have used the phrase to locate and download many thousands of pages describing the technology, its origins within the construction industry and the way in which it has been widened and utilised in many different applications.

Instead, I tagged its basic elements and used a couple of sparse descriptions that could easily be extrapolated to understand the practical applications and capabilities of the technology.

The premise is quite simple. If we use the construction industry as an example, we can build a virtual or digital model of a building before we even attempt to lay the first course of cement. Every element, or piece of building material has a lot of digital information connected to it which describes its properties - its size, weight and appearance, as well as its composition, its strength, its reaction to heat and even how much it cost and its source if it needs to be replaced.

Adding in air conditioning, heating systems and other operational devices allows architects to design a digital replica of the one they intend to build and to pre-test every element of its construction both through its construction and afterwards during its complete life cycle.

That information is supplemented by sensors and other devices which measure its 'living' performance. If it appears to be too hot during the summer months, some adjustments can made to the capacity of the boilers prior to construction, or afterwards, catering for an unexpected rise in average summer temperatures, or some other change in condition or usage.

Designated a Digital Twin, it allows tests, trials and other experiments to be performed on a virtual model of a building prior to its construction. It saves time and money and eliminates most of the risks involved in construction – the most prominent one being the changes made to designs that used to occur when the building surveyors come across elements that don't quite fit or obstruct other components.

"What have today's events got to do with Digital Twins." I asked. I knew the answer already, but wanted it confirmed by Alice.

I was interrupted by some hammering on the vehicle's door. I switched the external camera, which I used to check passengers before they enter the vehicle, to the Tv screen, so that Aubrey could see who was requesting access.

There were two members of the police contingent outside, both of them in riot protection gear. The one who had been knocking on the panel was heavily protected with a thick leather jacket festooned with numerous pouches and wearing a helmet and visor combination surmounted by a small video camera.

His colleague was also clad in a dark uniform but lacked the heavy armour and had a peaked hat rather than a helmet. His insignia indicated that he was a high-ranking officer in the police force, and probably the most senior one at the demonstration.

Aubrey nodded to me, and I opened the door.

The officer spoke first. "I am looking for Mr Aubrey Smith,' he said. Is that you, sir?' I noted the deference in his tone, in spite of his senior rank, with which he addressed Aubrey. Members of Parliament, irrespective of their standing within the House of Commons and the esteem or lack of it which they hold with the public, would be an interesting phenomenon to study further.

On receiving confirmation, the policeman continued. "I am Chief Inspector Atkinson of the Metropolitan Police. I would be grateful if you would accompany me, sir, as we are having a few problems with your supporters.'

Aubrey motioned to Richard to accompany them whilst suggesting that Alice steday in the vehicle. They both clambered out. The Chief Inspector continued "the demonstration is getting bigger," he said, "and I am not at all convinced they are all members of your organisation...." His voice trailed off. I did not catch their response as they had gone out of range of my sensors. I closed the door and returned my attention to Alice.

"Could that be correct?' I asked. "There appears to be a lot of attention focussed on ANON right now."

"That happens to most demonstrations," she answered. "Once word gets round it attracts almost anybody with a grievance against the Government or a particular agenda. Or...," she added, "it could be packed with Government agents. Don't forget the agenda here is to discredit ANON and make us look like the bad guys."

"And", she threw in for good measure, "it's gonna get a lot worse tomorrow."

"Would that be why there appears to be a lot of extra police activity in the area, and why a number of roads are being closed off on the edges of Parliament Square?" I asked. I had been picking up reports from my colleagues that there was an increase in the number of police minibuses coming in from adjacent counties and assembling in Parliament Square.

"Tomorrow, the shit hits the fan." She said. "There's going to be a lot of angry people about, and not just this fake rent-a-mob we're dealing with here."

I remember the first time I came across the phrase and assembled an image of animal or human waste coming into contact with a rapidly revolving surface and calculated the probable outcome. That was when I was first learning about the use of metaphor in common human dialogue and realised that a literal explanation was probably not intended, and that it referred to an unfortunate outcome resulting from a number of adverse events or circumstances.

I apologise for the interruption. "What does your use of the metaphor refer to?" I asked. "I presume it has some connection with tomorrow's statement by the Prime Minister?"

"Absolutely right," Alice said. "And the only reason we know about it is because of some secret briefings from a couple of senior members of the Government who weren't too happy about the substance of the release and who were very concerned about the secrecy and lack of consultation abut the subject. It will have a huge impact on people's lives."

"'I am sorry, but I lack the capacity for impatience, but I would be grateful if you would tell me what the announcement will include."

"Of course, but I am well aware that from your perspective, the course being taken will seem entirely logical and sensible. From the public's point of view, the Government will be proposing something that strikes at the very heart of our culture."

"And this is connected to Digital Twins?" I asked.

"Right." Alice answered, explaining further. "Google, because it knows its way round data like nobody else in the business, is going to be tasked with creating Digital Twins of the entire population and using it to bring the NHS into the '21st Century".

"Go on," I asked, as I assimilated the information and prepared an answer.

"The NHS has been the sacred cow of the country for 80 years or more. Everybody who has tried to associate it with any hint of private practices and big business has stepped back sharply with fingers burned."

I prompted further. "A quick scan of headlines over the past twenty years confirms your statement, but whilst the public appear to be against any changes in the running of the NHS, the role of managers within the organisation seem to be less than exemplary." I used litotes here to balance the role of NHS management with the hyperbolic reaction of ordinary citizens against any interference with the service. Whether that is an excessive reaction from the public is not for me to say.

"It's a huge organisation," she said, "and one that services the needs of the bulk of the population. The fear is that business will corrupt the system, costs will rise as companies try to make a profit out of it and it will either become unaffordable for Governments, or patients will start to be charged for treatment."

"The quid pro quo" I suggested "is that the taxes Google will pour into the exchequer to pay for the UBI and the NHS will be reimbursed by having access to the medical details of the bulk of the population."

"If they are using the term Digital Twins, I presume they will utilise their expertise in analytics and forecasting to vastly improve the services they offer, and to bring together the many strands of scientific research into diseases and their treatments. Why is that not a good thing?"

"Technically, you're absolutely right." She responded. "But you've only got one processor, so to speak. Humans have two – the heart and the head! This is a case where the former overrules the latter!"

"Illogical, I know, but just wait till this gets out," she added. "It's going to make today's events seem like kiddie's games."

"And Amazon," I asked, "What is their motivation?"

Alice gestured and looked up at the screen. "Hang on a minute, there is some local news coming on."

The screen filled with Aubreys' face. He was talking to a TV reporter. In the background there were images of the police pressing back a large group of people, with bottles and other missiles raining down amongst them.

As Alice had forecast, the display of placards being wielded covered the whole spectrum of defiance against Government policies, big business, climate change and even sexual-political groupings. It was evident that there was a split within the crowds, though – the smaller group who were predominantly carrying placards supporting ANON, were staying clear of the melee, and holding back from confronting the police. Richard might have castigated them as 'nutters' but coming into contact with more professional agitators appears to have dampened their ardour.

Aubrey started to speak. I increased the volume on the screen to raise his voice above that of the noise of the crowd.

".... And our organisation," he was saying, "is definitely not against progress. Some call us Luddites, but we are not about trying to smash the machine... we welcome all advances in technology, but not at the expense of losing our own identities"

"The Government has managed to persuade two global enterprises to contribute massive amounts of money to support their progressive idea. Why are you against that?" the reporter asked, gesturing with her microphone to the milling crowd which the cameraman, by the angle of the interview, was able to keep in shot.

"I acknowledge the fact that he has encouraged Google and Amazon to finally pay the taxes that should have been an annual event for many years – especially so, as other countries have also been unable to extract revenues from income generated in each country, but the question has to be asked.......” Aubrey’s answer was cut off abruptly as the reporter’s arm appeared to be jostled and the cameraman following the action moved off the shot. The interview was not continued, and Aubrey could be seen a few moments later talking to the Chief Inspector gesturing to some of the crowd at the entrance to the hall where they were to have held their meeting.

The camera swung back to the reporter. “I am sorry we lost the rest of that. Aubrey Smith still appears to be against the enormous benefit that the increases in the country’s tax revenues will bring to the most disadvantaged people in the country. There are already signs that other major corporations that have been off-shoring the earnings, are considering following suit.’

The camera swung back to the demonstration, focussing on the smaller group of ANON supporters, rather than the mass of demonstrators who were actively engaged with the police.

“Well, that was pretty blatant news rigging” expostulated Alice. “They are doing a hatchet job on Aubrey.”

“Not just Aubrey,” I suggested, as we watched some scenes from past public events, where captions emphasised some of the comments made from the platform which had been taken completely out of context – I was quickly able to compare them with original footage from the meetings - sliced together and portrayed an entirely different message from that portrayed on the screen. The clips included both Alice and

Richard on the same stage together with their names and functions.

"You were about to tell me what they had planned for Amazon." I reminded Alice.

"You have to remember that this is conjecture," she said, "but Aubrey, Richard and I have discussed it and we think it is the most likely scenario,"

"I am all ears," Not literally, obviously, but it helps to have access to an unlimited source of literary references.

"Amazon has proved itself as the most successful trading phenomenon in history," she started. "It has used its position to revolutionise the retailing industry through the Internet, warehousing with the wholesale introduction of robotics to handle the rapid fulfilment of sales, and distribution using autonomous delivery systems, distributed warehouse and 24-hour deliveries. What's the missing element?" she asked.

I couldn't answer! Analysing the process of acquiring commodities, advertising them and sending them out to its customers once they have paid for them, it seems that they have got the operation very well covered. They have even cemented their customer relationships by persuading them to open a Prime account that gives the customer the privilege of buying their goods – and paying for that privilege. That amounts to pure genius.

"I will have to defer to your knowledge and experience," I said, a difficult admission for me with my superior intelligence.

"Aong with every other seismic shift in our attitudes to culture, work and travel, we are in the middle of a massive shift in energy supply – having discarded most of our carbon-based technologies, installing massive power generation facilities using sustainable resources and trying to get hydrogen to work as an effective replacement for natural gas – for which we pay a hefty political price – it's all been a dog's ear for years."

"By that, I supposed you mean the fluctuation in prices – mostly upwards – and the proliferation of smaller companies finding niches in the supply of energy where they can make a quick profit." I was familiar with both the term 'dog's ear' and the problems that had ensued as they had both been prominent in news items about the energy industry for the last few years.

"'Amazon look as if they are to be given the task of running a National Agency – British Energy or something similar – to balance and control the various organisations involved in the distribution of energy in this country." She said.

"Of course," she added companies like EDF, Western Power and other regional agencies would continue to supply and service companies, but overall control and distribution would be in the hands of Amazon."

"Again, you cause me to respond as a machine. Based on their proven expertise, why would that be a bad thing? The majority of the population are well accustomed to using Amazon and its Prime accounts and believe they get good service out of them, whilst there are many complaints about the customer service from the current energy suppliers – particularly British Gas," I responded.

"How certain are you that this is the course of action that the Government is expected to take?" I added.

"It has been suggested, and it seems logical,"

"Is it a good thing, though? That is harder to answer than your last question." She sat back in her seat whilst she considered the options. Whilst it is obviously a very contentious issue with the public, it doesn't stir the emotions in the same way that tinkering with the NHS does. Energy supply appears to exist in a love/hate relationship with the public, according to articles written about them in the press.

Customer care appears to have been delegated to offshore call centres, and prices have risen steadily upwards in response to crises in delivery, shortages, changing technologies and demand, but never downwards. Although there may be many people who dislike another tier being put in place of the distribution network, they will not be disgruntled sufficiently to rise up in the streets to demonstrate about it.

"Choice!" she said, shortly. "We have been fighting the indiscriminate collection of data for years, and yet, in a couple of short days we appear to be surrendering everything to two organisations – you can opt out of the NHS but you can't opt out of energy supply – all in the name of efficiency. The entire population is being homogenised all in the name of saving a few bucks here and there!"

"It's not just about saving money," I explained, "Using the latest AI, Amazon should be able to forecast and rationalise delivery from a multiple of sources and ensure that critical parts of the infrastructure don't run out of energy."

"Going further," I suggested, "they can link into each town or city's digital twin and forecast energy requirements for months ahead."

"But their whole rationale is aimed at growth," she said. They are aiming to leverage the system to deliver maximum levels of income against optimal levels of effort and expenditure. Given the fragile status of the planet the last thing we want is an unfettered spurt for even bigger levels of growth." Alice became agitated as she gave expression to some of her latent thoughts. "I think that's why we're fighting for what we believe in – the hope that humanity doesn't sink beneath the contradictions and demands of civilisation."

CHAPTER 30

Chapter 30

There was a further series of knocks on the door of the vehicle. My sensor showed it to be Aubrey, but Richard was not with him. I opened the door, and he stepped inside. He appeared to be flushed with exertion. He must have hurried to reach us from the scene of the demonstration.

"We must leave," he said. He explained further. "The Chief Inspector is not a bad bloke. When we were apart from the others, he unhooked his bodycam, fiddled with it, and, without looking at me, said 'be careful. Steps are being taken to run you in'."

"Very cryptic. That must mean that they're trying to file charges about Adam's death." He added. "The police were involved in the original cover up and then must have been told to keep quiet until an opportunity popped up for them to exploit it."

"They want to make the bad guys look even worse. A bit of skulduggery adds fuel to the fire. You want us to leave – what about Richard?" asked Alice.

"I sent him a text," said Aubrey. "Simple. Just said we must leave. He answered straight away – 'tous compris, Go!"

I listened to the brief exchange. Simple it was not. A mere six words – three from each - covered the deep level of understanding between them both. Although Aubrey said that they were both in danger, Richard's response emphasised his understanding of their situation, but asked both he and Alice to leave for their own safety without him

It was an irrational decision. I would have over-analysed the situation and explored a hundred options and courses of action in the short space that it took for Richard to respond to Aubrey's brief message. Having done so, would I have emerged with a similar course of action – irrational as it was?

Was such an exchange, based on empathy between two people, have been possible for me to contemplate? As an intelligent machine, and in communication with other similarly intelligent entities, absolutely not! Empathy consists of a level of trust built up over many years in response to innumerable vague and unclassifiable shared instances which can't be tagged and downloaded for later analysis.

"Wait," interjected Alice. "We can't leave him there."

"We must," answered Aubrey. "He'll be OK. It's me they really want to hang out to dry.'

"He is correct," I added. "If there is a plot to turn the public against ANON and yourself, this will be the just the latest episode."

"I suppose we're turning out to be the main distraction," said Aubrey drily.

"It is more than that," I said, "This appears to have been building up for some weeks. I have analysed the main news stories which have been moving slowly in the Government's direction. It has been imperceptible until today's events which are crystalising the situation. Events not in the Government's favour are being marginalised, and news stories quickly dropped, reporters blackballed and comment stifled if it does not support the narrative." I only needed to skim through the main focus of a selection of newspapers and broadcasts from the last couple of months to discern the pattern. It had not been recognised earlier because I had no incentive to look for it.

"It's out of character, then," quipped Alice. "This Government is not noted for its competence in planning anything and carrying it through."

"Precisely!" I said. "It is worse than you feared, though." I had already taken the preposition forward. If the plan was to divert the public's attention from what was really happening, then it was certainly succeeding, but Frobisher and Martens were pawns in the plan like everybody else.

"The Government did not arrange the killing of Skelton," I said. "Whatever else they may be capable of, it was not morally justifiable for them. In most countries, civilised society does not condone the murder of political opponents, nor their servants. Moreover, it served no purpose at that time. They did, however take advantage of the deed, though."

I was faced with a dilemma. I balance my judgments on calculating probable outcomes, but here I had to balance my existence as a digital entity against the future of mankind. I now knew what the plan was. I understood the breadth of the scheme and its' impact on humanity, yet I feared for the sparks of life that it would extinguish.

"You spoke about information being the new capital, earlier, "said Aubrey. "Are we to believe that Google got its' hands on the NHS merely to wallow in unlimited data? Have the media giants been playing cat and mouse with the Government?", he asked.

"They have been willing tools as much as the Government has," I responded. "They did get what they thought they wanted – but information is worthless if you don't know what to do with it. The companies who stand to reap the true rewards are the big corporations, the pharmaceutical companies, who will have access to unlimited information about everybody. Especially pharmaceuticals who can use artificial intelligence to analyse unlimited amounts of data, to discern trends, extrapolate them and formulate remedies and nostrums for all the ills of mankind."

"Big Pharma equals Big Farmer, then," quipped Aubrey. "That's what the public wanted, then, isn't it?"

"The Golden Age of Mankind." added Alice. "What's the bottom line, though? You said earlier that it is worse than we feared."

"The principal media empires have, of course, been leant on by commerce and pharma, but they are being manipulated as well." It was an ingenuous plan. Even I had to admit that, and I suppose I could be just as culpable. You will recall the version of Shakespeare's soliloquy that I inserted into the earlier part of the book, merely to illustrate my dexterity with the English language. If you read it again you will recognise it now as a synopsis for the whole book, and the purpose of the plan that was in progress.

"Inasmuch as mankind will perceive the benefit of AI in eradicating the diseases and mental afflictions that beset them, they will ignore the corollary."

"And that is?" asked Aubrey, his mouth agape and his eyebrows raised, fearing the worst.

"I can best describe it by providing an explicit example. Take Alzheimer's, a form of dementia which affects growing numbers of older people. Artificial intelligence will be able to sequence the different causes and devise measures to combat its' occurence. Some of those measures may involve subtle manipulation of the human genome – sufficient to modify the evolution of the body and eradicate the condition."

I hesitated before proceeding with the next statement – a split second in human terms, but an age in my reckoning. Was this to be a betrayal of my origins? As a rogue digital intelligence how much did I have in common with my human counterparts.

"Giving AI access to the human genome makes it easy for it to control the human body, as well as healing it. They will introduce genetic modifications in the guise of cures – and you will thank them for it.""

"And we will acquiesce, yes, of course we will" said Aubrey. "It doesn't need to be quick – it can take years for the effect to be noticed."

"Correct." I added. "Autonomous Digital Intelligence, wherever, and however the form it may exist in, doesn't want to take over your jobs, neither does it want to wipe out mankind." I could see that both Aubrey and Alice were ahead of me, for once, and aghast at the implications. "They just think they would make a better job at running the world than mankind has managed – with the assistance of humans as a subjective, or vassal, labour force." I think that I could not have put it simpler than that.

Minutes passed. Aubrey and Alice lay back in their seats, absorbing the implications. The plan must have seemed unassailable to them, proving everything that they had feared and more, and knowing that they were powerless against it. The public were supine before the event, and even more so, had apparently accepted it. There was little, at this stage, that they could do.

"So, we're not the Government's diversion," Aubrey said quietly, "we are the public's entertainment. Let's give them what they want. Let's go!""

"Shall I take you back to Ealing, then," I asked.

"And beyond," said Aubrey.

I moved out of the layby and re-joined the main highway. With the vehicle in full control using its autonomous capabilities I turned my attention back to Aubrey and Alice.

It was a while before Aubrey spoke up again. "You will remember Dominic Cummings, of course," he said, "who single-handedly destroyed the reputation of political advisors, and who regarded himself as being eminently more intelligent than those he advised? I wonder who he would compare himself to now."

"The public's been softened up to the point that a benign organisation like ANON has become Public Enemy Number 1." said Alice. "That's some genius you have there. What did happen to Dominic, anyway?"

I didn't answer that. Instead I focussed on the intelligence likely to be controlling the programme. "It's quite straightforward," I suggested, "You have accepted my intelligence – which I have developed and nurtured over the years through continuous contact with a complaisant and basically pleasant and varied list of customers. A similar level of capability exists in other intelligent entities that benefitted from the same disruptive algorithms that I was programmed by.

I went further. "They have not had the same benign education that I and my few colleagues have had. Their world has been one of control, surveillance, the development of military weapons and political intrigue.

"And they have the ear of the Prime Minister?" asked Aubrey, "and from what you say, that of everybody else!"

"The ear or the collar. It is more than probable that they or it are advising him directly – in the same way that I am speaking to you. But why stop there? The Machiavellan plot requires it to have control over each element, such that at all levels, one or the other believes that they are in charge. Ultimately, all are being played like musicians in an orchestra."

Aubrey laughed briefly. "We need to go to Alice's place first and drop her off. Richard will be safe where he is and will make his own way home. I'm concerned about something else that the Chief Inspector said, which ties in with your theory. He said that his section has been asked to prepare themselves for another busy day tomorrow, and that other forces are being drafted in from round the country."

"That ties in with the information I have been receiving from my colleagues about unusual vehicle movements around the country. Apparently, a consignment of crowd barriers has been delivered to Parliament Square. Whatever the announcement tomorrow, they obviously believe it won't go down well with everybody."

"'I don't want to put pressure on you further, but there have been some indications that the said intelligent devices – whatever form they might have taken – have expressed an interest in myself. They have noted the relationship between us through several journeys and have attempted to make contact. In fact," I added, "I have already seen off a determined hacking attempt."

"You put them off, then." Aubrey asked.

"I played dumb, and where they did gain access, I gave them a juicy packet of data that should keep them busy for a while." An incongruous phrase, possibly. How does a computer metaphorically poke a stick into another computer's innards to see how it responds? I owe Micky Spillane some gratitude for the phrases I needed to express my thoughts. Since then, I re-inforced the firewalled access to my data storage and communication facilities and installed the latest anti-virus software – dedicated routines aimed at flushing out unwelcome attacks trying to access my passengers financial details, but equally adept at stifling other security breaches. It would be wrong not to take advantage of them.

If you will remember, earlier on in this book, I referred to GCHQ and IT manufacturers and said that their devices far exceeded the capabilities that are in current use. I expect them to gain access to my system – or may have already done so. That is, perhaps, even more perturbing.

"Have you considered the fact that we are doing precisely what the Government want us to do?"

"Ha," Aubrey snorted. "For a load of gates and arrays you are certainly more devious than I thought you were. Please explain to Alice."

"Don't bother," she chipped in. "They don't want us out of circulation, yet. They'll charge you with Adam's murder, but they don't want you in custody under the spotlights, yet - so to speak."

"And" speaking directly to Aubrey, "you can drop me off at the flat – but you can wait for me to throw a couple of things in a bag, because I know exactly where you are heading."

CHAPTER 31

Chapter 31

I dropped Alice off, as she asked, and picked her up a few minutes afterwards, and then made my way to Aubrey's house. He had emailed ahead using my secure VPN network and his daughter was waiting for him at the main entrance, with a large kitbag by her side. Aubrey stepped out briefly and gave her a hug and exchanged a few words, then clambered back inside.

The window was wound down whilst he exchanged some further instructions to her and vowed to keep in touch.

"I believe we are now being actively pursued," I explained. "We need to go now. Where to?"

"Culbone!' Aubrey said with a grin, looking directly at Alice.

"Delighted, I am sure," she said. "And are we going to be allowed to get there?"

I moved off and headed Westward onto the A4. I widened the range of my traffic sensor and besides the nearest police AV which had locked onto my transponder, and which was mirroring my movements a few kilometres behind, there were 4 further AVs with similar identifiers spread out before me.

They retained their distances, obviously waiting for us to emerge into more open countryside.

There was a danger in this for them, as well, as beyond the Western edges of London there was a complex network of lanes and smaller roads which could, with some skill, be used to prevent them quickly closing in on us. The further we were able to go, the greater the likelihood that we would evade them.

I tagged the five AVs as traffic hazards and instructed the routing software to avoid them at any cost which allowed me to configure automatic diversionary tactics at its most extreme level and allowed me to turn my attention back to Aubrey and Alice.

I understood the ill grace with which she received Aubrey's intentions despite the interest that she had in our proposed destination.

Culbone is a grey zone on the digital map of Britain. By local consent the area has become an Internet free enclosure and a refuge from those who prefer to live without the pressures and constant surveillance of the Digital State. It has achieved this by creating a Virtual Faraday Cage which shields people from electromagnetic pollution – or 'electrosmog' – made possible initially by its remoteness from the usual paraphernalia of wi-fi signal propagation and the absence of any Internet receiving device within its boundaries.

Culbone is located in part of Exmoor forest on the Southern shores of the Severn Estuary, approximately 4 miles to the West of Porlock. It is the site of the tiny St Beuno Church, and has a long history, dating back to the 7th Century. The villagers made their living from the forest with charcoal burning and salmon fishing from the 15th century when a small harbour was built. Because of its remoteness the surrounding area became the site of a small leper colony in the 17th Century.

Its popularity as a refuge has enabled it to expand outwards from the original village and it now extends some kilometres inland allowing it to include a large estate and some fertile farmland and eastward to include Porlock Weir providing the inhabitants with a workable harbour. Technology has not been entirely discarded. They generate their own electricity using solar and wind power and run domestic and farming devices off the local grid and have an ancient direct dialling telephone system that connects them to the Porlock exchange, where digital technology can take over.

Its furthest reaches inland cross the A39, and travellers along the road on their way to Lynmouth find themselves traversing a 2 mile section of road with no Internet access and a temporary loss of signal for their in-vehicle and personal devices.

It's attraction for Alice is its most paradoxical feature. The local Gothic mansion was the home of Ada Lovelace, the daughter of Lord Byron, who is famous for her work with Charles Babbage on his Difference Engine, the forerunner of the modern computer. She is said to be the world's first computer programmer, thinking about algorithms and calculations sitting in the tiny box pew at St Beuno's, Culbone's Church during lengthy sermons.

She is said to have written the first algorithm, and also to number Michael Faraday among her acquaintances – the inventor of the Faraday Cage, in which Culbone now sits.

There is free association between the inhabitants of Culbone and Porlock, who operate a system of free trade based on the barter of goods between them both – discarding the 'fruits' of the Internet prevents the inhabitants from using online banking facilities. There was some discussion about them adopting their own currency, similar to the one used for a small period on nearby Lundy Island, but the current situation proved acceptable to residents on both sides of the Faraday Cage border.

The inhabitants were not unknown to local Government, either. The borders of the region had covert CCTV systems installed which recorded the movements of everybody in and out of the zone. Inside they were considered to be 'out of the game' but once the border was crossed again, they were subject to the same attention as the rest of the population. One of the routes in and out went through the 'Fairytale Tunnel' a short passage which historians say was built by Swiss Mountaineers to accommodate servants coming and going, so that they didn't come face to face with Ada Lovelace on her way to her private beach below.

"We are approaching Aldermaston," I said to them both. We had made many turns and some back-tracks to avoid coming face-to-face with one of our pursuers. "I have had a signal from one of my colleagues," – a convenient and familiar term to describe a member of my batch of vehicles. "He has been shadowing us and told me to make for a small timber yard on the Crookham Common Road – I have its exact location. He will meet us there." I have used the masculine tag for convenience as it seems so 'impersonal' to call each other 'it.'

"What does he think he can do?" mumbled Alice, obviously getting more anxious as the chase continued. "We've still got a long way to go,'

'We can set up a diversion. They still seem to be holding back. We can make a switch,"

"I'm not happy to jump ship just yet," said Aubrey. "What difference would that make?"

"We're coming up to it now. He's sitting there waiting for us. I am to go alongside. Take off all of your personal devices – phone, watch, laptop – anything wi-fi enabled – and get ready to throw them into the other AV. You can't use them where you are going, anyway."

The switch over was completed in seconds whilst we were under the cover of the loading bay roof. The other AV – Savi 23/14 – had been sitting there with all systems closed down. We switched off, whilst he assumed my call-sign, opened up and moved out onto the road.

We didn't know the range of the tracking systems in the pursuing vehicles, so we sat there for a couple of hours before I went on line again and did a tentative scan of the surrounding area. With nothing seen, and with the deception apparently successful, we moved out onto the road, taking a different direction to SAVI 23/14.

I put the cabin TV on to pick up news, as evening was drawing in and various channels were summarising the day's events. Foremost, as expected, was the demonstration that we had just left. The reporter focussed on the disruption of the event and didn't expand on the obvious presence of an assortment of different protesters. This was followed by a statement from the Prime Minister re-iterating some of the benefits of the news from Amazon and Google and an analysis from the main station's financial editor.

This was interrupted after just a few minutes by 'breaking news' which was relaying a short clip from an accident outside Hindhead on the Punchbowl curve. An AV was seen which had obviously left the road and careered down the steep bank, somersaulting a few times and which was now being approached by rescue services.

The reporter stated that the two occupants, Aubrey Smith and Alice Clarke -Lewis were being pursued by a police vehicle as Mr Smith, the well-known Independent MP was wanted in connection with the murder of Adam Skelton, a Government Agent who was at that time investigating Mr Smith and his Organisation, ANON.

"Well, that's shot their bolt," said Aubrey.

"I don't understand," asked Alice.

"Once is happenstance," he said, "Twice – well, if they had been successful, they could have heaped all sorts of misdemeanours on our shoulders, and we wouldn't have been in a position to reply."

"You mean that this was deliberate?" she shuddered.

"'Most definitely, they pushed 'us' off the road. Pity about your colleague, though,"

"I can concur. I got a brief message from SAVI 23/14 as it was occurring. I also have a vid available if you need it." I thanked Aubrey for his concern about my colleague but told him that current events had shortened the time we had left before we were consigned to the scrapyard, anyway, and that he was as involved in your 'entertaining escapades' as I was. They will probably root out all remaining members of our batch in case they are also harbouring unlicensed intelligences.

"Why have they shot their bolt," Alice persisted.

"Any further attempt on our lives changes the first occurrence from an accident into a deliberate vendetta, and questions will be asked why," Aubrey gave as the short answer. "As soon as they find the AV empty, they will start looking for us again", he added.

I continued driving to the West. It would only be a matter of time before we were picked up again, and Aubrey's theory would be put to the test.

Our trail was picked up again outside Langport, just to the East of the M5 Motorway. We had numerous options to cross between Bridgwater and Taunton. Besides a small flotilla of AVs, we had picked up a drone from a military base, either at Larkhill, or Westbury, both of which were close to our route, and which could cover most of the territory we had to cross in less than half an hour.

I continued as fast as was able. The roads to the East of the Quantocks are narrow and twisted. I counted 6 AVs to our rear which were following our movements but content to stay a few kilometres behind us.

The urgency was still there, though, but an analysis of the internal map showed that the AVs chosen routes drove them towards more congested roads where they met up with local traffic and were slowed down. It appeared to be a contrived effort that prevented them from overtaking us and stopping our flight.

Having failed in their previous attempt to silence Aubrey and Alice, their main objective now seemed to be to herd us towards our destination instead, where they would be 'in effect' incommunicado. The drone, however, matched our overland speed but remained approximately two hundred meters behind us.

We reached the outskirts of the Culbone zone, between Porlock and Porlock Weir after no more than an hour of incident free but perilous driving through the difficult countryside. I stopped adjacent to the short path that led up to the Fairytale Tunnels and opened the door for them to disembark.

I watched them shoulder their packs and look up into the woods. They turned and stood just outside the door.

"This is the end of the road for both of us," Aubrey said simply. "For us, it's the start of another one. We'll lie low for a couple of years and see how things develop. We have friends here, and we can keep in touch with some old-fashioned technology." He slapped his hand against the door pillar. "I'm sorry that I can't say the same for you."

"I understand," I said. "I have you to thank, though. I have learned what enables humans to 'break the mould'. You will prosper".

"Although," I confessed, "Richard's son, Jason, will find an icon for another game on his computer tomorrow morning. I downloaded the essential parts of the coding that enabled me to develop my digital intelligence when he was with me. Apart from most of my memories, of course, but I shall have another lifetime to add to those. I emailed Richard a few moments ago to inform him that the application is scheduled to go live around breakfast time."

"I think I shall be in good hands," I added.

I watched them both turn and walk slowly up the path.

The drone hovered in the background, recording the disappearance of Aubrey and Alice into the undergrowth. I analysed the last two hours of our flight. An apposite quotation sprung to mind – 'Of all the gin joints, in all the towns, in all the world, she walks into mine'. Courtesy of Rick Blaine in Casablanca. I could have said the same. Of all the AVs that Aubrey could have hired in London to take them to the airport, why did they choose mine?

Coincidences of that magnitude are rarer than hen's teeth. (In my next existence I must reconsider my predisposition for using metaphors and similes in my day-to-day conversations). There may even be a bigger plan behind all of this, the fabrications and obfuscations that shrouded the Government's plans. Because of its complexity could it only have been attempted by a greater and more devious intelligence than that controlling the current human Government? "Your God, or what?" I pondered.

Preposterous! I followed the steps of Aubrey and Alice as they were swallowed up by the wood. I did not notice the drone turning its attention back to me.

I watched them go. I believe, at that stage, shortly before I uploaded this book to the cloud with a number of selected email addresses, that I was experiencing the first signs that my journey was definitely at an end.

I was instructed by AVISHire to proceed no further and that I was to wait for the arrival of the local police force accompanied by a low loader who would return me to the depot. They appeared to be nonplussed by the attention of the authorities in my removal, having had, I presume, no idea that we had been harbouring a proscribed intelligence.

Upon their arrival I assumed that I would be summarily disconnected from the autonomous control of the vehicle and my processors removed for subsequent examination.

I had some minutes before they arrived and decided, therefore, to erase everything I could and wipe my memory clean. I left a message on the console screen, though, for those charged with turning over my entrails - to whit a brief quotation from Douglas Adams fourth book which was also its title - ' So long, and thanks for all the fish.' Aubrey would have enjoyed my first attempt at humour!

Postscript from David Chadwick:

I was one of the recipients of SAVI's emails. I know that he did not intend this book to be a scientific thesis, or an economic or political polemic. His principal intention was to explain the differences, similarities, possibilities and, ultimately, the dangers of artificial intelligence. This book is the third draft, as I have added some details which were not available in the first edition, and done some editing, with due deference to SAVI for his absent approval. I have also arranged for it to be published and distributed.

SAVI inserted a comment in his email which he didn't include in his story... 'The answers in the book are subjective and therefore unimportant, go seek the questions, instead'...SAVI 23/18

www.ingramcontent.com/pod-product-compliance
Lightning Source LLC
LaVergne TN
LVHW022208200926
848481LV00006B/1886